The Angels of Christmas

The Angels of Christmas
Hearing God's Voice in Advent

The Angels of Christmas
978-1-7910-2425-3
978-1-7910-2426-0 eBook

The Angels of Christmas DVD
978-1-7910-2429-1

The Angels of Christmas Leader Guide
978-1-7910-2427-7
978-1-7910-2428-4 eBook

Also by Susan Robb

Called: Hearing and Responding to God's Voice

Seven Words: Listening to Christ from the Cross

SUSAN ROBB

The Angels of Christmas

HEARING GOD'S VOICE IN ADVENT

Abingdon Press | Nashville

THE ANGELS OF CHRISTMAS
HEARING GOD'S VOICE IN ADVENT

Library of Congress Control Number: 2022937436
978-1-7910-2425-3

MANUFACTURED IN THE UNITED STATES OF AMERICA

For Don and Fran,
ordinary angels who have made an
extraordinary impact on countless lives

CONTENTS

CONTENTS

INTRODUCTION

What images first come to your mind when you think of Christmas? Is it of your family gathered around the Christmas tree on Christmas morning? Hanging ornaments together and recalling the delight of seeing again your favorite decorations that had been boxed away for the rest of the year? Memories of sitting atop Santa's lap as a child, or watching the joy on your own children's faces as they carry on that old tradition? Or perhaps singing "Silent Night" in a darkened sanctuary during candlelight services on Christmas Eve with friends and family? Whatever images of Christmas we think of first, as Christians our imaginations do not take us far before visions of angels appear in our minds. For most, thoughts of Christmas almost always include gossamer images of winged angels appearing to Mary, Joseph, the shepherds keeping watch over their flocks by night, and, if we really dig deep in our memories, to Zechariah, the father of John the Baptist. (Yes, Zechariah and his wife, Elizabeth, and the angel that brings them the good news of their son's impending birth, are an integral part of Jesus's birth story as well.)

We cannot relate the Christmas story, watch a Christmas pageant, or even walk city streets or the aisles of otherwise secular department stores during the Christmas season without encountering images of angels. Some of our most enduringly popular Christmas movies, such as *It's a Wonderful Life* and *The Bishop's Wife,* have angels in central roles. They appear not with wings but as everyday human beings sent to earth to teach the meaning of Christmas and offer hope to distracted, misguided individuals who have lost their way—to bring hope and light into the bleakness of their lives.

Angels are not unique to the Christmas story. They appear throughout the Bible during significant moments in the history of God's people. However, their role as God's messengers of hope, peace, salvation, direction, warning, and especially of Jesus's identity, make their words in the birth narratives of Jesus messages we all need to hear, heed, and claim today in this season of Advent.

The word *Advent* comes from the Latin word *adventus,* which means "coming." Specifically, it referred to a visitation by the emperor—an event that required people to make special preparations. During Advent, as Christians have done for centuries, we prepare and wait expectantly for the coming of our King; for the birth of the Christ Child in the midst of our lives and hearts once again, for the return of Christ, whose arrival was announced by John the Baptist, inaugurated at Jesus's birth, and evidenced in his life on earth; and for the consummation of his kingdom.

The angels in the stories of Jesus's birth are significant to our time of waiting and preparation in Advent. That's really the reason for this book. Angels are not just beautiful decorations for our trees. They are more than the coolest costumes for the Christmas pageant. But it's dangerously easy to reduce them to such roles, even in our formal celebrations. Think about the Christmas hymns we know well. Notice how many of them include, or even begin with, the angels:

> "Hark! The herald angels sing, 'Glory to the newborn King.'"

> "Angels we have heard on high, sweetly singing o'er the plain."

"It came upon the midnight clear, that glorious song of
old, from angels bending near the earth to touch their
harps of gold."

The one role angels have in each of these hymns—singing—is not
mentioned at all in the Gospel stories. I don't wish to burst any bubbles
here, but in the Gospel accounts angels don't sing. They speak. Of
all the most familiar Christmas hymns, the only one I can recall that
makes this key distinction begins like this: "The first noel the angels
did *say* [emphasis mine] came to certain poor shepherds in fields where
they lay." The word *noel* is a borrowing from French that refers both to
news and to a birth. In the Middle Ages it came to mean specifically
the news of the birth of Jesus. The angels in the birth narratives of Jesus
aren't actually depicted as singing. Yet, we refer to the words of praise
that Jesus's mother, Mary (Luke 1:46-55), and Zechariah (Luke 1:68-
79) offered at the announcements of their sons' births as "songs," due
to their beautiful poetic nature. The words of the angelic host in Luke
2 have similarly captured our imaginations—and those of the writers
of our favorite hymns—as a song of the good news of Christ's birth. So,
with no bubbles burst, we can join with the angelic chorus in "singing"
the good news of Christ's birth!

This book attempts to bring our focus during Advent back to the
central role of angels as bringers of news. The word *angel* derives from
the Greek *angelos*, meaning "messenger." The angels of Christmas came
to deliver important messages to people who were hoping for God
to intervene in a mighty way, both in the fears and darkness of their
personal lives and in their world. One of those angels reminded the
doubt-plagued recipient of his message, "I am Gabriel. I stand in the
presence of God" (Luke 1:19)—implying that the messages the angels
bring are to be heeded as carefully, and met with the same awe and
wonder, as messages that come straight from God. More than that:
messages from God through the angels demand a response from us, by
word or action.

Introduction

So, over the course of this book, we will look at the messages delivered by the angels regarding the birth of Jesus. We will carefully read, study, and, hopefully, ponder them in our hearts, as Mary did, not just for the four weeks of the Advent season, but far beyond. We will also examine how these human recipients responded to the messages from God. And I hope we will ask ourselves not just how we would have responded had we encountered the angels in these gospel stories, but how we recognize and respond to the angels that I believe are still in our midst.

The angels of Christmas still bring "good news of great joy for all the people," including you and me.

Just as they did two thousand years ago, the angels of Christmas still bring "good news of great joy for all the people," including you and me, and the tidings they bring can allay our own fears and bring "great joy" into a hurting world desperately in need of hope (Luke 2:10). Upon hearing such news, whether it's for the first time or the thousandth time, the question for us today is, How we will respond?

Angels in the Bible

The appearance of angels in the Hebrew Scriptures didn't necessarily conform to the way we depict angels in Christian art and in our Christmas pageants.

When the parents of John the Baptist, Elizabeth and Zechariah; and Joseph, Mary, and the shepherds encountered angels, they could process what they were seeing and hearing based on what they knew of the appearances of heavenly beings in their own Scriptures, which we know as the Old Testament. So, to better understand their reactions, we need to understand how angels were presented in Bible stories that predate Jesus's arrival by many centuries.

While the word *angel* in Greek, as noted earlier, means "messenger," in Hebrew, the language of the Old Testament, no single word precisely corresponds to the word *angel*. Instead, there is a rich and varied vocabulary to describe these celestial beings. They are called "sons of God," "heavenly beings," and "hosts" (see, for example, Genesis 5:22; Job 1:6; Psalm 103:21). They don't necessarily appear with wings and wearing white robes. It's not always even clear who they are. Genesis 18 describes an occasion when three "men" show up at the camp of Abraham and Sarah. Displaying hospitality was an essential part of ancient Near Eastern culture, so in this narrative, Abraham invites the visitors to stay, while Sarah prepares them a veritable feast. After they tell the couple that they will have a son in their old age, Abraham must realize that he is in the presence of heavenly messengers. The text abruptly shifts in tone, and "the LORD" begins to speak. Was God there all along, as one of the three? Were these men angels? It's not clear, but the author of Hebrews hints that they were angels (Hebrews 13:2).

When Abraham is preparing to sacrifice his son Isaac—a command that, according to the narrative in Genesis 22, comes directly from God—the order not to follow through is given by "the angel of the LORD," who then reaffirms God's promise to make Abraham's descendants as numerous as the stars. There's similar blurring between God and angels in the stories of Abraham's grandson Jacob. In Genesis 28, as he camps overnight, Jacob sees a stairway to heaven—one of those "thin places" where our realm and the heavenly realm come close—with angels going up and down. Then the LORD appears directly and speaks to Jacob. Later, when he is once again camped alone, on his way back to face his brother, Esau, Jacob wrestles all night with a stranger, who gives Jacob a new name, Israel (which means "wrestles with God"), and whom Jacob understands to have been God.

Introduction

Angels function in a variety of ways as messengers. An angel comforts the slave girl Hagar after she runs away from Sarah. As with Jesus, centuries later, angels announce the coming births of Isaac, Ishmael, and Samson (Genesis 18:10; 16:10; Judges 13:2-5). Angels commission people to a specific task (think of the angel of God who appears to Moses from the burning bush). They speak God's words to prophets, redirect or guide someone's actions at a critical moment, or act in ways that offer protection for God's people.

The list could go on, but we will discover that the angels in the birth narratives of Jesus functioned in many of these roles as well. Their appearances in Matthew and Luke's Gospels are meant to echo similar or parallel stories from the Hebrew Scriptures, connecting the old stories of God's faithfulness and action in the history of Israel with God's continued faithfulness and new action through the life of Jesus.

But angels can also be frightening bringers of bad news, not "good news of great joy for all the people" (Luke 2:10). God sends a heavenly being, a *cherub*, with a flaming sword, to prevent Adam and Eve from returning after their expulsion from the Garden of Eden (Genesis 3:24). Two of the angels who visit Abraham's camp travel on to Sodom, where they encounter his nephew, Lot, who also shows them great hospitality and invites them to stay overnight in his home. Instead of welcoming these strangers, the men of Sodom try to abduct the "men" from Lot's home to bring them violent harm. So, the angels bring about the destruction of the city as punishment for its wickedness against the strangers in their midst, and for its known prevalent injustice. An angel with a drawn sword blocks the path of the pagan diviner Balaam; at first, only Balaam's donkey can see the menacing angel, but then the Lord opens Balaam's eyes, and he bows his head to the ground in fear and submission (Numbers 22:21-34). Given these stories, it is little wonder that Zechariah, Elizabeth, Mary, Joseph, and the shepherds might have been perplexed and frightened by the angels' appearances— and why they (like the women who encountered them at Jesus's empty tomb that first Easter morning) needed to hear the reassuring words, "Don't be afraid."

Are Angels Real? And Does It Matter?

In conversations I've had with people through the years, I have found that some are wholehearted believers in angels, while others' sense of logic does not permit their embracing that sort of belief in supernatural beings. For the latter group, angels belong in the same category as Santa Claus, Rudolph the Red-Nosed Reindeer, and the Easter Bunny. I find that some of these people ascribe the appearance of angels to a literary device used to support the biblical author's theological message; others have walked away from the faith entirely because the Bible includes angels as well as historical, archaeological inaccuracies and supernatural occurrences that do not mesh with their knowledge base and reliance on reason. And that is tragic, because we need to understand that the biblical authors of the first century and earlier were not writing to an audience that expected absolute historical accuracy. They were writing in the literary styles of their day, to people who viewed events through the lens of their own cultures. In particular, the Gospel accounts of Jesus's birth that we will read in Luke and Matthew seek to help us find the points of connection between the good news of the birth, life, death, and resurrection of Jesus to God's saving action in the stories of Israel, and to the Gentile world into which the early church had spread.

If you're skeptical about the identity of angels, you're not alone. Even in Jesus's era, faithful people were divided on the belief in angels (see Acts 23:8). But whether you are a devoted believer, a wistful hoper, one who sees the inclusion of angels in biblical narratives as mostly literary device, or purely a skeptic, you can still experience through their messages the grace, power, hope, awe, and mystery of what God was and is doing in the world through the incarnation. This study is not an apologetic for the reality of angels. Instead, I intend to focus on the role of angels in the birth narratives of Jesus, what their messages tell us about the One born in Bethlehem, and his role in the salvation of the world. And that's good news for all people!

Each of the four chapters in this book, corresponding with the four weeks of Advent, connects us to human beings who received messages from angels: Zechariah and Elizabeth; Mary; Joseph and the magi; and the shepherds. As we explore together the richness of these stories, we'll pay particular attention not just to what God's messengers said but also to how these people responded to the message.

That's where the stories connect to us. God did not stop attempting to communicate with human beings once the Bible was written. Just because we don't read stories from our own time of people seeing angels filling the night sky, or encountering men in dazzling white robes, that doesn't mean God no longer sends messengers to interrupt our everyday existence. As you'll read in this book, some people are convinced they have been in the presence of an angel whose message brought them hope and strength or even changed the direction of their lives. Others have wondered, after an unexpected encounter with a stranger, whether they might have been visited by an angel. I love the spiritual advice that the writer of Hebrews, reflecting this sensibility, gives to his readers: "Do not neglect to show hospitality to strangers, for by doing that some have entertained angels without knowing it" (Hebrews 13:2).

Angels in the World

Whether or not you believe in the existence of divine beings who can assume human appearance, here's what matters most, what I want you to take from this volume: God still reaches out to us through messengers, whether they're heavenly or purely human, complete strangers or people we know well. There are times in your life and mine when, in the words of the old spiritual, "God is trying to tell you something." How can we orient ourselves to those moments, so we can grasp what God is saying? Once we comprehend the moment and the message, how will we respond? And finally, how will we perform our own part in this unending story of the arrival of the Prince of Peace, God arriving to experience life as one of us? How will we convey what we have heard and seen to the broken places and beleaguered people around us? How will we spread the good news to all people that the kingdom is here, and we are invited to live in it together as members of the beloved community? How do we go from being shepherds who receive the good news, to serving as angels who share it, who allay fears and provide guidance for God's people?

I'm so glad you've joined me on this journey of discovery this Advent season as we open these beautiful narratives in the Gospels of Matthew and Luke. As we prepare our hearts for the birth of the Christ Child once again in our lives this season, and as we await his return with eager anticipation, may we all listen closely to what God has to say to us through the messages of the angels of Christmas. As we hear anew these ancient stories, my hope is that we come away from this study transformed by the wonder and joy of Christ's birth—and by a renewed sense of purpose in response to their messages. May we, too, make connections between what God has done in the past, not only in the history of God's people, but in our own lives as well, and may we embrace whatever new thing God is calling us to through the gift of the One who came to bring light and life into the world at Christmas.

CHAPTER 1

Standing in the Presence of God

Gabriel and Zechariah

CHAPTER 1

STANDING IN THE PRESENCE OF GOD

Gabriel and Zechariah

In the days of King Herod of Judea, there was a priest named Zechariah, who belonged to the priestly order of Abijah. His wife was a descendant of Aaron, and her name was Elizabeth. Both of them were righteous before God, living blamelessly according to all the commandments and regulations of the Lord. But they had no children, because Elizabeth was barren, and both were getting on in years.

Once when he was serving as priest before God and his section was on duty, he was chosen by lot, according to the custom of the priesthood, to enter the sanctuary of the Lord and offer incense. Now at the time of the incense offering, the whole assembly of the people was praying outside. Then there appeared to him an angel of the Lord, standing at the right side of the altar of incense. When Zechariah saw him, he was terrified; and fear overwhelmed him. But the angel said to him, "Do not be afraid, Zechariah, for your prayer has been heard. Your wife Elizabeth will bear you a son, and you will name him John.

You will have joy and gladness, and many will rejoice at his birth, for he will be great in the sight of the Lord. He must never drink wine or strong drink; even before his birth he will be filled with the Holy Spirit. He will turn many of the people of Israel to the Lord their God. With the spirit and power of Elijah he will go before him, to turn the hearts of parents to their children, and the disobedient to the wisdom of the righteous, to make ready a people prepared for the Lord." Zechariah said to the angel, "How will I know that this is so? For I am an old man, and my wife is getting on in years." The angel replied, "I am Gabriel. I stand in the presence of God, and I have been sent to speak to you and to bring you this good news. But now, because you did not believe my words, which will be fulfilled in their time, you will become mute, unable to speak, until the day these things occur."

Meanwhile the people were waiting for Zechariah, and wondered at his delay in the sanctuary. When he did come out, he could not speak to them, and they realized that he had seen a vision in the sanctuary. He kept motioning to them and remained unable to speak. When his time of service was ended, he went to his home.

After those days his wife Elizabeth conceived, and for five months she remained in seclusion. She said, "This is what the Lord has done for me when he looked favorably on me and took away the disgrace I have endured among my people."

Luke 1:5-25

Christmas Eve of 2001 is as clear in my mind as if it were yesterday. I had been attending seminary just over a year and joined our home church staff a few months earlier. Highland Park United Methodist Church is very large and at that time had a clergy staff of nearly twenty ministers. As in all churches, Christmas Eve was an "all hands on deck" event, offering sixteen services at our main campus alone. We often rotated associate ministers and those in the ordination process in liturgical roles in various services, but I was in what you might call my rookie year. So, I was shocked and honored beyond belief when our senior minister invited me to serve as liturgist in three of our Christmas Eve candlelight services. There were many other, more qualified people to choose from. How could I have been so fortunate to have been selected for this honor?

The invitation, and the evening itself, were among the most humbling, sacred, awe-inspiring, and (to be honest) fear-inducing moments of my early ministry. Christmas Eve is such a holy night that it always fills me with a certain awe. As a minister, you want everyone to experience the presence of God in a mighty way, and you desire to represent God to those you are serving in such a way that God's grace and love come shining through your words, presence, gestures, and actions. That responsibility should strike a healthy fear and sense of awe in all of us. It certainly did for me on that evening. But there was also the fear of messing up. No one wants to fall on her face, either literally or figuratively, in front of several thousand people. In preparation for the evening, I was fitted for and ordered my first clergy robe. I also wrote and rewrote prayers and rehearsed climbing the stairs to the pulpit and reading the Christmas scriptures over and over and again. Finally, I practiced how the candles representing the light of Christ should be lit (just before the singing of "Silent Night"), when they should be shared by walking the aisles and lighting others' candles (on the first stanza), and finally, when they should be lifted (last stanza).

When Christmas Eve finally arrived, I carefully donned my vestments for the first time, exhibiting an outward sign of God's unique call and claim on my life. It truly was a holy moment for me. I had served the church in many capacities before, but this act was symbolically fulfilling a new call and a new way of living out my faith.

The presence of God was palpable for me that evening. Toward the end of the service, as is always the case on Christmas Eve, all the lights were turned off in the sanctuary. The only light remaining was the tiny flame of the Christ candle on the Advent wreath reaching up into the massive darkness of the cavernous Gothic sanctuary. From the

Christ candle, the senior pastor lit his candle, then shared that light with me. We then slowly walked the center aisle, sharing the light of Christ with a person on each pew we passed. Each person who received the light shared it with the next person in the pew, and slowly, slowly, light began to flicker and replaced the retreating darkness. The senior minister and I raised our candles and began to sing, "Silent night, holy night, wondrous star, lend thy light." Everyone else in the room joined us, filling the sanctuary with the light we all received from Christ. Tears filled my eyes (as they do every year now during the third verse of "Silent Night") but gone was any fear that I had brought into the room that evening. My angst had been replaced with wonder, joy, and peace. I sensed the same was true for everyone present that evening.

I had come seeking to serve God that night feeling honored, humble, awestruck, and a little afraid, and I left feeling even more honored, humble, awestruck, and full of wonder and joy. That range of emotions, it seems to me, was similar to what happened to the priest Zechariah as he came to serve God in the Temple over two thousand years ago.

An Unbelievable Day in the Temple

When we ponder the Christmas story, Zechariah isn't the first name that typically comes to mind. Actually, his name might not come to mind at all. We are more likely to remember his wife, Elizabeth, whom Luke describes as a relative of Mary, the mother of Jesus. But Zechariah and Elizabeth both hold an important place in the story of Jesus's birth.

As the scripture reminds us, Zechariah and Elizabeth lived in the time of King Herod the Great. The author of Luke, who informs his readers that he seeks to provide "an orderly account" of the life of Jesus (Luke 1:1, 3), also loves to set the historical stage for us. Zechariah and Elizabeth, like all of the Jews in Judea in that era, lived under the oppression of the Roman Empire and Herod, its despotic puppet king. Zechariah was a priest from the order of Abijah, and his wife was a descendant of Aaron, Moses's brother.

Part of the law given to Moses on Mount Sinai ordained that Aaron be a priest, along with all of his male descendants from that time forward. Elizabeth is from Aaron's line, but so is Zechariah. According to 1 Chronicles 24, Aaronic priests were ordered into twenty-four divisions, each named for Aaron's twenty-four sons, and they took turns serving at the altar in the Temple, much as our clergy do at church. This ensured that there was always a priestly presence at the Temple and that responsibilities were fairly distributed to each division of priests. Zechariah is from the order of Abijah. It was expected that women born into priestly families would marry priests.

Why is the point about the priestly lineage of Zechariah and Elizabeth important for Luke? Because he wants to underscore for us their righteousness. They have impeccable credentials. They lived "blamelessly" concerning matters of piety and upholding the law of Moses (Luke 1:6).

"But they had no children, because Elizabeth was barren, and both were getting on in years" (v. 7). Right now, bells would be ringing in the heads of first-century Jewish readers of this story. If there is an old barren couple mentioned in the Hebrew Scriptures, what can we expect? You guessed it. God will definitely be intervening in their lives in a miraculous way to give them a son. And when God does this, the baby born will be no ordinary child. Invariably, the son is given for an extraordinary purpose. Isaac marks the beginning of the "great nation" that God promises to Abraham and Sarah (Genesis 12:2). Jacob, whose name is changed to Israel (by a "man" he wrestles with all night), becomes the father of the twelve tribes of Israel. Samuel becomes a priest, judge, and prophet who anoints the first two kings of Israel. So, as readers, we know that something incredible is about to happen, but when and how? Let's see.

Zechariah is one of the priests whose section was called to be on duty at the Temple. He and Elizabeth live in the hill country near Jerusalem, but there would have been accommodations at the Temple to house the priests during their time of service there. Zechariah is no doubt honored that it is finally his division's turn to go and serve at the Temple. I can imagine that he packs his best linen robe and prayer shawl to wear while he's in service. Who knows? He may have even had a new one made. He has practiced the words to his prayers and his role. But when he arrives in Jerusalem, he is shocked that out of all of the priests there, when the lot is cast to see which priest should go into the holy place alone to represent the people before God, he is chosen. We don't know if this is the first occasion when this honor has fallen to him, but given the large number of priests, at the very least it must have been a rare occurrence, and the person on whom the lot fell (much like dice to us) would have been seen as God's choice.

Angels were not always bearers of good news.

Taking his role seriously, Zechariah approaches the altar in the holy place to make his incense offering on behalf of the praying worshipers gathered in the courtyard just outside. Suddenly, an angel appears on the right side of the altar. As noted in the introduction to this book, angels were not always bearers of good news. Not knowing if this is good news or bad, Zechariah's first impulse is fear. And then the angel speaks calming words: "Do not be afraid, Zechariah, for your prayer has been heard" (Luke 1:13). Everyone who is visited by angels in the story of Jesus's birth—Zechariah, Joseph, Mary, and the shepherds—will hear those same opening words: "Do not be afraid."

The angel goes on to declare that he and Elizabeth will have a son. They are to name him John, which means, "God is gracious." The angels tells them how much joy this child will bring to Zechariah and his wife, and also to "many...for he will be great in the sight of the Lord" (vv. 14-15). And then there are detailed instructions for how the child should be raised.

As someone steeped in Israel's Scriptures, Zechariah would have known this was hardly the first time that God had acted graciously for childless couples. He knew the story of Abraham and Sarah, to whom God had given a child in their old age. He'd have known the anguish of Hannah, who was the object of taunting over her infertility and so distraught that she promised that if God would give her a son, she would dedicate the boy to the Lord's service (see 1 Samuel 1:1-2, 6-7, 9-11, 27-28; 2:1-10). In particular, he'd have known how these various figures reacted when faced with God's blessing them with a special child of promise. Abraham falls on his face. Sarah laughs. Hannah breaks into a "song" of thanksgiving.

Why the Gospel Writers Tell the Story Differently

Before we go further, let's take a moment to consider why we even have the story of Zechariah and Elizabeth in our Gospels. After all, we read nothing about them except in the first chapter of Luke. What's going on here?

The story that we present in Christmas pageants is so familiar that we think of it as a unified narrative in the Gospels. It may come as a surprise to some that only two Gospels, Matthew and Luke, tell us anything about Jesus's birth, and each of them is quite different in nature and content. For example, Matthew mentions nothing of the shepherds. Luke mentions nothing of the wise men. Understanding the audience and purpose of the various Gospel writers can give us insight into why these witnesses often choose to emphasize different details about Jesus's life and ministry—and perhaps lead us to deeper insights into what their messages offer to us.

Mark, author of what is believed to be the first written Gospel, opens his story with a fully grown John the Baptist appearing in the wilderness. The earliest Christians would have had an institutional knowledge of who Jesus was. They also believed that Jesus's return was imminent. Thus, Mark may have felt no need to describe the details of Jesus's birth. The urgent message is: "Believe and respond now."

The author of John, who wrote in the late first century and was the latest of the Gospel writers, may have skipped over Jesus's birth because his emphasis was on helping people grasp Jesus's oneness with God the Father. John presents the arrival of Jesus in cosmic terms ("In the beginning was the Word, and the Word was with God, and the Word was God"), with a lyrical and poetic parallel to Genesis 1 conveying Jesus's preexistence with God (John 1:1). In the person of Jesus, God engaged in a second bold and marvelous act of creation, becoming a human being and living alongside us. Even if John had knowledge of a birth story, its inclusion in his Gospel might muddy his theological intent.

Matthew, author of the most Jewish of the Gospels, is probably writing to a community of Jewish Christians. For several decades, these followers of Jesus were widely regarded as another of the many groups within Judaism. By the time of Matthew's writing, sometime after the destruction of the Temple by the Romans in 70 CE, these Jewish Christians are being turned out of their synagogues. For this audience, who are experiencing doubt and confusion as to whether they can still cling to the stories and scriptures of their past, Matthew presents Jesus as the new Moses and the fulfillment of the Jewish Scriptures. Like Moses's, Jesus's life is threatened as an infant by the ruling powers. Like Moses, he is sent to save God's people. That's one reason it's important for Matthew to give us the story of Jesus's birth.

Luke, meanwhile, is writing primarily to Gentile Christians in the wider Mediterranean world. He, too, emphasizes the importance of Jesus's connection to, and continuation of, the traditions of the past while embracing the full inclusion of *all* people. The author of Luke, who also penned Acts, is believed by many to be one of Paul's missionary companions. If so, he would have heard Paul's message that within the community of believers, there were no distinctions between Jews and Gentiles, male and female, enslaved and free persons. He would have seen how people at the bottom of Greco-Roman society, women and slaves, flocked to these early Christian communities. So, while Matthew's audience, interested in proof of Jesus's royal kingship, reads of the wise men, Luke chooses to emphasize a different detail: that the word of Jesus's birth came first to poor and humble people. And it's no surprise, given that Luke includes so many stories of Jesus's interactions with women, reinforcing the message of spiritual equality, that he chooses to focus on the angel's visit to Mary and her amazing response.

For both Matthew and Luke, including Jesus's birth narratives in their Gospels would also have satisfied the curiosity of the growing number of Christians who, due to the span of time and geographical distance, would not have had prior knowledge or memories of Jesus's life. But most important, the inclusion of these birth narratives and the messages the angels deliver in them offers additional support to the theological and Christological claims of the Gospel writers—to elaborate on what the resurrection proved. The resurrection brought to light what had been true from Jesus's infancy (or as John would declare, from before creation). So, the infancy stories are actually an infancy gospel.[1]

Everyone's Prayer Has Been Heard

"Do not be afraid... Your prayer has been heard." Those words are not just for Zechariah and Elizabeth, who have been longing for a child

11

their entire married lives. They are also for the crowd that has been left praying outside. The people in the crowd, representing the nation of Israel, have prayed for generations for a Messiah to deliver them from the oppression of their enemies. They sought deliverance from slavery under the Egyptians, and God sent Moses. Later, they prayed for deliverance from the oppression of the Assyrian, Babylonian, and Persian empires, and from the stranglehold of Hellenistic leadership and the murderous reign of Antiochus Epiphanes IV (175–164 BCE). Now they seek God's help in delivering them from the crushing oppression of the Romans.

Zechariah and Elizabeth's deepest prayer will be answered, just as it was for Abraham and Sarah, for Isaac and Rebekah—and for Hannah. Hannah, like so many other women mentioned in the Old Testament, was barren. Her husband, Elkanah, adored her, but Elkanah also had a second wife—one who had been blessed with children and who constantly taunted Hannah for her apparent infertility. God graciously answered Hannah's prayer for a child. Her son, Samuel, was the answer not only to Hannah's prayers, but also of a nation that felt spiritually barren and constantly provoked by its enemies, the Philistines.

As priest, Samuel turns the hearts of Israel back to their God. As a judge, he leads them into battle when needed and keeps them safe from their enemies. As a prophet, he anoints the first two kings of Israel, Saul and David, as God instructs. It was customary for prophets to anoint kings by applying oil to their heads, signifying that they were chosen by God.

The baby who is about to be born to Zechariah and Elizabeth, like Samuel (who was also raised as a Nazirite), is going to be a beacon of God's grace, turning the hearts of those who are praying toward their God and each other, to ensure that they are ready to recognize and receive God's greatest gift when it arrives: their Savior and King. Just as Samuel anoints the heads of the first kings of Israel, John the Baptist anoints Jesus's head with water in his baptism, signifying God's anointing of him with the Holy Spirit for his ministry on earth.

The answered prayer of Zechariah and Elizabeth is a blessing and an answered prayer for others as well. I imagine that if the parents of Franklin Roosevelt and Winston Churchill, Martin Luther King Jr., and Marie Curie prayed for them when they were born, they had no idea that their children would later become answered prayers of a world engulfed in war, a country plagued by systemic racism, and countless others desperate for a treatment for cancer.

What prayers have you had answered that wound up being a blessing for others as well? Years ago, my husband and I prayed for God to lead us to a volunteer opportunity where we could both serve together—one that we would both enjoy and in which we would find fulfillment. That opportunity came in the form of our church's involvement in building homes for Habitat for Humanity. God answered our prayer, but in the process also answered the prayers of many people who were desperate to raise their families in a decent, affordable home. No doubt, your answered prayer to find the right fit for a volunteer opportunity was someone else's answered prayer for food, clothing, an affordable home, or a compassionate listening ear. Perhaps your answered prayer to find the right job became someone else's answer to prayer for a great mentor. Perhaps you didn't know that when your prayer to find the right house for your growing family was answered, it was also an answered prayer of other parents who hoped their children would find warm and welcoming friends and a safe, nurturing place for them to gather.

After Zechariah hears the astounding news that Elizabeth is going to bear a son, it's not surprising that he, like Abraham and Sarah, might have doubts about how this could happen. Sarah's response to the news that she would bear a child in her old age was to laugh. Was she laughing for joy, or because she found the angel's news laughably absurd? I don't know, but Zechariah doesn't laugh. Instead, he asks for a sign: "How will I know that this is so?" (Luke 1:18).

It may be that the angel expects that one who is so well versed in the Scriptures—one who is so faithful and pious and righteous—might

13

fall on his face in gratitude to God for answering his prayer in the same way that, as he already knows, God has answered the prayers of his ancestors throughout Israel's history. But Zechariah seems to ignore the good news of the past and cling to the same doubts that seem to plague our own minds. "Does God really still care about what's happening in my life and in the lives of those around me?" we ask. "Does God really still answer prayer in such magnificent ways? How could God make something that seems so impossible happen? I need more proof."

I Stand in the Presence of God

In answer to his question, the angel offers Zechariah some significant information to aid his doubting mind—along with a huge sign.

First the information: "I am Gabriel.... Let that sink in, Zechariah" (Luke 1:19, paraphrased). The old priest would have known exactly who Gabriel was. God sent Gabriel to Daniel to help him interpret one of his visions (Daniel 8:16), and later as an answer to Daniel's prayer, to give him insight and understanding (9:21). As if Zechariah needed a reminder, Gabriel says, for emphasis, "I stand in the presence of God, and I have been sent to speak to you and to bring you this good news" (Luke 1:19). Because Gabriel stands in the presence of God, Zechariah should know that the angel's words come from God's own self.

Now the sign. Because Zechariah disbelieves the good news Gabriel has shared with him and wants a sign, Gabriel will give him one: Zechariah will be struck mute until John is born.

Wait! The laughing and incredulous Abraham and Sarah weren't struck mute. That doesn't seem quite fair, does it? But we do find that Daniel became "speechless" for a short time after Gabriel interpreted his vision (Daniel 10:15)—not from doubt but perhaps from awe. Maybe being struck mute for his disbelief was as much to help Zechariah—and us—make the connection to Daniel as it was a punishment.

I wonder if there aren't times when we have all been struck mute by doubt. Maybe there have been times when we could have been giving thanks for God's good news, but instead our lips remained unmoved because we weren't quite sure we could believe it. Or maybe we've been struck mute out of fear that others will doubt or mock the good news we have experienced in our own lives. Have you ever been there? Sadly, I have.

I wonder if there aren't times when we have all been struck mute by doubt.

Zechariah will be unable to speak as long as Elizabeth is pregnant. Nine months is a long time. As I have pondered Zechariah's gestational season of silence, it has dawned on me that perhaps the sign Gabriel inflicts upon Zechariah is more of a gift than a punishment. Maybe it will be a great gift for him to not be able to speak as he ponders what Gabriel has proclaimed; how God has miraculously worked to bring life and light to the middle of his people's yearning, barrenness, and darkness in the past. Maybe it will be a gift for him to silently watch his wife's formerly barren belly swell and move with the life God will provide within. Maybe it will be a blessing for him to just listen in silence to what God has to say to him.

In that silence Zechariah might have recalled another lesson from Israel's past: a time when God's prophet, Elijah, has been threatened with death by Queen Jezebel. People are worshiping idols throughout the land, and other prophets are being killed. Elijah, who has just witnessed the power of God in a showdown on Mount Carmel against the prophets of Baal, flees for his life into the desert wilderness after Jezebel vows to kill him (1 Kings 19). An angel provides food for him along the way. Elijah is hiding in a cave when "the word of the LORD" comes to him and tells him to stand on the side of the mountain while God passes by. First, there is a wind strong enough to tumble boulders. Then there's an earthquake, then a fire. The LORD appears in none of these.

Finally, God speaks to Elijah in the "sound of sheer silence" (v. 12). God asks him, "What are you doing here, Elijah?" (v. 13). Read it with the emphasis on the last word: "What are you doing *here*? I need you back in Israel, to speak and witness for me." Amid the sound of silence, Elijah is able to gain clarity. He understands his mission, what God is calling him to do—and then he does it. I'd like to think that Zechariah's quiet period helped prepare him for his role in understanding and carrying out his mission. When we are surrounded by silence, we may discover, if we listen, that we are in the presence of a great teacher.

Maybe it could be a gift for us to find some extended time in the Advent season to be speechless, to listen—to God, to friends, to the yearnings of others—and to ponder God's goodness in our own past. What if we blocked out some of the noisy chatter in our lives over those four weeks to listen to what God may be saying to us? Maybe that pondering could bring us a season of greater belief, hope, joy, and peace. Maybe it could help prepare us for the work God calls us to do.

When Zechariah finally emerges—people at the Temple had to have wondered why it was taking him so long—it's obvious from his gesturing and inability to speak that he's had a powerful experience of God's presence. They believe something extraordinary has happened. In several months many of them will understand that their wait was worth it and that their prayers for a deliverer were answered.

Zechariah arrives at the Temple that day humbled and honored to have been chosen to serve the God he loves. He leaves humbled, honored, awestruck, and overwhelmed at being in the presence of a messenger who stands in the presence of God. He leaves believing the angel's message. He leaves knowing what Sarah and Hannah learned centuries before, that with God all things are possible. He leaves knowing what Abraham learned—that he is blessed to be a blessing to others. His answered prayer will in some way be an answered prayer for many.

When Zechariah returns home, even though he cannot speak, my guess is that the excitement revealed in his animated gestures conveys to Elizabeth that this has been no ordinary visit to the Temple. It was not just another day at the office. God is at work in their lives.

This Is What the Lord Has Done for Me

"After those days Elizabeth conceived." The good news comes to pass! But Elizabeth goes into hiding for five months. Why? Maybe she just wants to savor this moment alone with Zechariah for a time, or maybe she wants to ensure that she has an unmistakable bump before going out in public. Or perhaps she needs time and solitude—as Zechariah's imposed silence provided him—to process what God is doing through her.

In Elizabeth's society, children were considered a blessing from God, and being a mother conferred a certain status. While producing children was not regarded as part of a woman's religious obligation, being childless nevertheless could be a source of anguish.

I have known people who have been told by fellow Christians in their church community that suffering their family had experienced—a child born with a congenital illness, for example—was God's punishment for sin. (Thankfully, in my experience such occasions have been rare.) Christianity teaches no such thing. Judaism doesn't teach it either. Nevertheless, this point needs to be emphasized because in Elizabeth's day and in our own, some people try to impose such judgments on God's behalf. Elizabeth may have experienced it, just as people do today. Perhaps she heard quiet murmurs as she passed other women shopping in the marketplace or saw questioning glances and shaking heads. Because I have seen blameless people believe they are somehow in part to blame for unfortunate and unavoidable situations, it's possible for me to imagine that Elizabeth might have borne a burden of self-imposed guilt.

Even Jesus's own close followers were not immune to sometimes thinking, wrongly, in terms of blame. Chapter 9 of John's Gospel recounts an occasion when the disciples came upon a man who had been blind from birth. Was it because the man had sinned? they asked. Or was it because his parents had sinned? Jesus immediately corrected them. "This is not about sin," he said. Then he showed them the proper response to suffering: he healed the man, who then joyfully told everyone around what Jesus had done for him.

That is how Elizabeth responds to the news that her infertility is over. A great emotional burden has been lifted from her through this miraculous blessing. She is filled with joy! When it's obvious that she is pregnant, she gives thanks to God, "This is what the Lord has done for me when he looked favorably on me and took away the disgrace I have endured among my people" (Luke 1:25). Her and Zechariah's years of yearning, their years of tears and disappointment that bound them so closely together, have come to an end.

Have you ever felt like Elizabeth? Have you experienced a time of barrenness in your life (either physical or spiritual)? If so, you are not alone. You are feeling what millions of others have also felt. You are experiencing what Elizabeth experienced. And only from the depths of such despair is it possible to understand the Everest of joy that comes with the kind of amazing news that Elizabeth finally receives.

There are others whose "barren times" never come to an end. The blessing or deliverance they yearned for never arrived. Are such persons less worthy somehow of God's mercy, as some might judge whose first response is to assign blame? Of course not. The answer, as the Gospels always show us, is to follow Jesus's example: Heal the sick; reach out to the hurting; be the conveyor of God's love and grace. Be an angel.

The Birth and Naming of John the Baptist

If you know Luke's story well, you know that Mary is next on Gabriel's visitation list. But let's skip ahead a bit in the narrative, to Luke 1:57-80, the birth of Zechariah and Elizabeth's child promised by the angel. As the angel predicted, Elizabeth gives birth to a son, and all her neighbors and family are as joyful as she is over his arrival (something also foretold by Gabriel). Many of them gather eight days later to celebrate John's circumcision. As part of the ceremony, the attending rabbi turned to Elizabeth—the only one of the parents who could speak—and asked, "What name is given this child?" Everyone behind her was saying "Zechariah, of course!" Not in all areas, but obviously in theirs at the time, it was customary to name a firstborn son after his father. Many of us do the same thing today. We all know someone who is a "Junior" or "the Third." Our son's name has been passed down for four generations in our family.

"No," Elizabeth answers to those around her who assume the baby's name will be Zechariah. "He is to be called John." It is the name given to him by Gabriel, given to him by God. Everyone turns to Zechariah, who confirms Elizabeth's answer on a writing tablet. The crowd is amazed. And true to Gabriel's word, the sign that Zechariah had asked for is lifted. He hasn't spoken in nine months. His last words expressed doubt. His next words are nothing but praise!

The gathered crowd, perhaps many of the same ones who were at the Temple on the last day Zechariah could speak, realize that this child not only has been sent by God as a gift to Zechariah and Elizabeth, but that he is also destined for something great. "What then will this child become?"

Notice here how the roles suddenly shift. Zechariah has had nine months to contemplate the message that Gabriel brought to him. Now, filled with the Holy Spirit and able again to speak, it is Zechariah who becomes God's messenger to the people. The message of praise comes pouring out of him like a song.

Zechariah's Song

Zechariah's song has come to be known as the Benedictus. It is named for the first word of Zechariah's song in Latin: *Blessed*. "Blessed be the Lord God of Israel, for he has looked favorably on his people and redeemed them" (Luke 1:68). In his beautiful song—reminiscent of Hannah's song (1 Samuel 2:1-10), and Mary's song, the Magnificat (Luke 1:46-55)—Zechariah gives thanks, not only for what God has done in his life, but for what he now knows God is doing in the life of his nation. His gratitude looks beyond what his son will do and toward the One his son, John, will point others to: "a mighty savior" from "the house of his servant David" (Luke 1:69). Zechariah's words pour forth with strength and authority, recalling the promises of God and the words of the prophets from the past. His son will "go before the Lord to prepare his ways" (v. 76).

I love the way Zechariah ends his Spirit-filled song: "By the tender mercy of our God, the dawn from on high will break upon us, to give light to those who sit in darkness and in the shadow of death, to guide our feet into the way of peace" (vv. 78-79).

Light has broken into Zechariah's and Elizabeth's darkness, but it is also beginning to break into the lives of those in their nation who are living in the darkness of political oppression and poverty. Elizabeth's all-but-dead womb has brought forth life out of God's graciousness and power. Light is about to dawn on those who also sit in the shadow of death, to guide our feet in the way of peace.

We all experience our own personal darkness, whether it's the darkness of worry for the health and security of our children, parents, family members, and dear friends, or the darkness of our own addictions, financial insecurities, failing health and relationships, or physical or spiritual barrenness. Additionally, we as a nation have been living in the darkness of a global pandemic that, as of this writing, has claimed more than one million American lives, perhaps including some of our own dear family members and friends.[2] Health-care workers' spirits are being crushed by the relentless bombardment of critically ill patients and death. We remain surrounded by the darkness of political divisiveness, the plague of racism, and the constant strain of global tensions and the fear of looming war. So, we pray for light to shine in our darkness, for a glimmer of hope, for a moment of peace in our lives, in our nation, and in our world.

We all experience our own personal darkness.

The Gospel writers meant for us to find ourselves in this story. Nowhere is this more evident than in the original ending of Mark's narrative of Jesus's resurrection (Mark 16:1-8). As in the other Gospels, Mary Magdalene and other women come to the tomb early on Easter morning. They discover that the stone sealing the tomb has been rolled away, and a young man dressed in a white robe tells them the amazing news that Jesus has been raised. Additionally, he tells them to go and share the news with the disciples that Jesus has been raised and will meet them in Galilee.

But the three women are clearly still so traumatized from witnessing Jesus's brutal, torturous death, still so shrouded in the deep darkness that has come over their lives, that they cannot process what the angel is telling them. As Mark describes it, "terror and amazement had seized them" (16:8). And so, despite the angel's words, "Do not be alarmed" (v. 6), they run away and tell no one.

Eventually, the women find their voice and fill the role of God's messengers, as the eleven verses that apparently were added later to the end of Mark explain. Perhaps, as some scholars think, those final verses

21

had been part of the story all along and somehow were lost in early copies of Mark, then recovered. Or perhaps, as most believe, the writer ended the story abruptly so that we, as readers, would ask ourselves, "What would we have done in that situation? What will we do when we are faced with fear of sharing the good news? When we are rendered mute with doubt and fear?"

These are questions that we may ask of all encounters with angels, from Elijah to Zechariah to Mary Magdalene to our own time. How will we respond? What will we say to others? Will we run away in fear, like the women on that first Easter morning, or react with disbelief, like Zechariah? Or will we, also like the women at the tomb, overcome our fears and the darkness that surrounds us through faith, find our voice, and tell the world what God is doing?

In the middle of our darkness, whatever that may be, God is preparing us for a light that leads our feet into the way of peace. God is preparing us to *be* a light that leads others to peace. God is preparing us to be a light that *brings* peace. It was so for Abraham and Sarah, for Isaac and Rebekah, for Hannah and her husband, for Zechariah and Elizabeth, and for you and me. May we, like Zechariah, find our voice and proclaim the message of the angel: Blessed be the God of Israel, who is at work, in ways we cannot see, in ways we can scarcely imagine, to bring light into the darkest times and places. In response to this news and what it means for a hurting world, how can we keep silent?

ANGELS GATHER AMONG US

Roberta, a member of my Bible study group, had driven her husband to MD Anderson Cancer Center in Houston, where he was to receive a lifesaving stem cell transplant. Before the transplant could take place, however, her husband required a very high-risk surgery. The doctors were honest as they told Roberta and her husband, Tom, that his chances of surviving the surgery were less than 50 percent.

Other than Tom's medical team, Roberta knew no one else in the hospital, and she'd had no conversations with others. Knowing the odds were not in her husband's favor, Roberta sat alone at a table in the waiting room while he was in surgery, laid her head down on the table, and began to sob. After a few minutes, a woman she had never seen before approached and introduced herself. She said that she and her mother had recently flown to Houston from Egypt, and her mother was having surgery that day. Then she reached out and touched Roberta's hand and said, "I just came over here to tell you that your husband is going to be okay." Roberta later said that when the woman touched her hand, a complete sense of peace washed over her, and her words and her voice filled Roberta with a deep sense of assurance and comfort.

Hours later, Tom came out of the surgery—alive. He made it through the critical hours of the night, and by the next day it was apparent that he would be able to receive his stem cell transplant in the near future. Roberta asked the nursing staff if they would lead her to this woman's mother's room so she could properly thank her for the words that brought her through the ordeal with a sense of peace. However, none of the nurses she spoke with had seen anyone fitting the woman's description, and they insisted that no one from Egypt had been admitted to the hospital.

Later that day, Roberta asked her husband's surgeon if he knew anything about the woman and her mother. The doctor affirmed the medical staff's assessment: "We don't have anyone here from Egypt." He went on to say, "We get stories like this all the time here at MD Anderson. You've just experienced an angel sighting!"

Sometimes angels appear in our lives in such a way and with such an impact that it's difficult to tell if their presence is human or divine. But one thing is certain: whether the angels we experience are of human or divine origin, the Divine is always at work in and through these messengers to offer assurance, guidance, comfort, peace, love, and protection to God's children.

CHAPTER 2
Let It Be
Gabriel and Mary

CHAPTER 2

LET IT BE

Gabriel and Mary

In the sixth month the angel Gabriel was sent by God to a town in Galilee called Nazareth, to a virgin engaged to a man whose name was Joseph, of the house of David. The virgin's name was Mary. And he came to her and said, "Greetings, favored one! The Lord is with you." But she was much perplexed by his words and pondered what sort of greeting this might be. The angel said to her, "Do not be afraid, Mary, for you have found favor with God. And now, you will conceive in your womb and bear a son, and you will name him Jesus. He will be great, and will be called the Son of the Most High, and the Lord God will give to him the throne of his ancestor David. He will reign over the house of Jacob forever, and of his kingdom there will be no end." Mary said to the angel, "How can this be, since I am a virgin?" The angel said to her, "The Holy Spirit will come upon you, and the power of the Most High will overshadow you; therefore the child to be born will be holy; he will be called Son of God. And now, your relative Elizabeth in her old age has also conceived a son; and this is the sixth month for her who was said to be barren. For nothing will be impossible with God." Then Mary said, "Here am

I, the servant of the Lord; let it be with me according to your word."
Then the angel departed from her.

Luke 1:26-38

If we had followed the order of Luke's writing and not skipped ahead to the birth of John the Baptist in the previous chapter, it would be quite easy to see that Luke leaves us having witnessed the angel Gabriel offer the good news that Zechariah and Elizabeth will have a son who is destined to be great, and with a jubilant Elizabeth who has been savoring her long-hoped-for pregnancy. Ever the orderly, detailed writer, Luke likes to insert time lines into his stories. It is the sixth month of Elizabeth's pregnancy, and now Gabriel has another mission to complete. This time he is directed not toward the Temple in Jerusalem but to a young peasant girl living ninety miles north of Jerusalem in an insignificant village of no more than four hundred people. In fact, this hamlet in Galilee is regarded so dismissively that when Philip, who had become a follower of Jesus, went to his friend Nathaniel and said to him, "We have found him about whom Moses in the law and also the prophets wrote, Jesus son of Joseph from Nazareth," Nathaniel asked a bit incredulously, "Can anything good come out of Nazareth?" (John 1:45-46).

But Gabriel appears in this hamlet, and to this unsuspecting young woman, with news that will one day stand the world on end. While the location of Gabriel's appearance to Zechariah was clearly stated—in the Temple, on the altar of incense, which would have been in the holy place (though not the Holy of Holies)—we have no idea where Mary is when the angel breaks into the quiet of her unassuming life. Gabriel visits Zechariah in the midst of his work, in the day-to-day routine of his priestly responsibilities, although in the most spectacular and holy of places. I suspect that Gabriel does the same with Mary.

She may have been in the middle of milking the goats, mending her brothers' tunics, or collecting vegetables from the garden. According to

Catholic tradition, she might have been drawing water from the village well, which sat over an underground stream and served for centuries as the main source of water for those who lived nearby. That well in Nazareth is now called Mary's Well.

Whatever Mary is doing, she has no earthly idea that she is about to be chosen to play one of the most distinctive roles in human history. She is about to find herself in the company of a select few women in the history of Israel who overcame a physical inability to conceive a child through the grace, power, and initiation of God.

Luke lets us in on a secret before Gabriel speaks. The woman he is about to visit not only lives in Nazareth, but she is also a virgin, engaged to a man named Joseph, who is "from the house of David." In those days, marriage involved a two-stage process. First was the engagement (or betrothal), which worked much as it does today, except that these engagements were legally binding. Often, the match was negotiated as a contract between families when the bride-to-be was quite young, maybe even still a child. In the eyes of the community, a betrothal legally bound the couple, but the marriage wasn't completed until the woman moved from her father and mother's home to that of her husband. Mary is a virgin. Luke's use of the term emphasizes not only Mary's youth but also the holiness of what is about transpire.

Luke makes sure we know that Mary's betrothed is from the ancestral line of David. It's one of his many reminders of how Jesus's story connects to the history of Israel and the promises God made to the people. David was the greatest king to occupy the throne in Israel. Through the prophets, God promises David that from his family line, God will raise up a son whose throne will be established forever (2 Samuel 7:12-16; Isaiah 9:7). There had not been a Davidic king in Israel since the Babylonian exile, almost six hundred years before Jesus was born, and it was widely believed that the Messiah would be a king from David's lineage (see Isaiah 11:1). This had been the hope and prayer of the people for centuries. Now, the angel announces to a teenage girl that the prayer is about to be answered, and she is to fulfill the role of the new king's mother.

Finding Favor with God

Gabriel startles Mary by declaring, "Greetings, favored one! The Lord is with you" (Luke 1:28). Perhaps to some readers this announcement is reminiscent of a story in the Old Testament: an encounter between a messenger from God and Gideon. As recounted in the Book of Judges, Gideon is threshing grain in a wine press for fear that this work, if performed in an open field, would attract the attention of Midianite raiders who have been terrorizing the land. Gideon is startled and uncomprehending when the angel says to him, "The LORD is with you, mighty warrior!" (6:12). Gideon wonders if this is a joke. After all, as he explains to the angel, he is the least mighty person in the weakest clan of one of the smallest tribes of Israel. Why would the angel call him a mighty warrior? Why would God's messenger tell him that he, lowly and fearful Gideon, is to be the leader God will use to rescue Israel from the Midianites? The news that comes to Gideon is like the incredible news that Gabriel brings to Mary: through her, a savior is to come into the world—and not just any savior but the Son of God. Anyone would be jarred by news like that.

Have you ever been so deep in thought or so engrossed in what you were doing that you were completely startled to hear out of nowhere, "Hey! What are you doing?" Did you jump? Were you frightened? I imagine this is a bit of what it was like for Mary—except this interrupter is no ordinary person, and his greeting is strange. Gabriel may have been enthusiastic and excited about greeting Mary. However, Mary was "perplexed" (Luke 1:29). Other translations say she was "troubled" or "greatly troubled." Perhaps she was a bit afraid, like Zechariah. So, Gabriel attempts to quiet those fears.

"Do not be afraid, Mary, for you have found favor with God" (v. 30).

This messenger from God, just as he did with Zechariah, knows her name! And he repeats that she is favored by God, that God is with her. Does Mary sense what Zechariah had to be explicitly told—that Gabriel stands in the presence of God? I'd like to think so.

What does it mean to be favored by God? What has Mary done to deserve this celestial visit? Some interpret Gabriel's address to mean that God found Mary to be extraordinary; that she was favored because she was so good. Catholics believe that Mary was favored by God because she was born sinless (how, they reason, could a sinful human being have become the mother of one who was born without sin?) and remained a virgin perpetually. Their tradition holds that Jesus's brothers and sisters were products of an earlier marriage involving Joseph. While there is no scriptural basis for either of these views—no mention of a previous marriage by Joseph or anything to suggest that Mary was somehow different from other humans—they do suggest how Christians over the centuries have wrestled with that question of what it means to be favored by God.

Others believe that Mary is favored exactly because she is ordinary and of humble circumstances, like most of us. God's favor upon her, God's presence with her, is a gift. No doubt she grew up in a pious Jewish home, praying for the hope of Israel, and would be a good choice to mother the baby who was to come, but out of all of the ordinary young women in Israel, God chose her.

This view fits with much of the rest of Luke's gospel, which focuses on how Jesus made a point of reaching out to "the least and the last" (see Matthew 20:1-16; 25:31-45). Mary is a peasant girl in an out-of-the-way village that is regarded, even within the region of Galilee, as undistinguished and unimportant. Later in his Gospel, Luke wants readers to know that Jesus declared that he had come to bring "good news to the poor" (4:18). That includes lepers whom Jesus encounters and sightless persons who are reduced to begging by the side of the road, and women who are suffering from years of hemorrhaging or being bent over in pain. But in the wider Roman world that Luke may have traveled with Paul, the early church found enormous appeal among women and slaves, two huge groups of people who occupied the lower rungs of their society. They flocked to the message that their lives were of equal value and importance with those who were rich and powerful—that, within the body of Christ, there were no distinctions between male and female, slave and free, Jew or Gentile (Greek) (see Galatians 3:28, among others). Could that message be part of what Luke is implanting here, at the beginning of his Gospel? Is Mary favored precisely because God's good news—the radically countercultural news of the gospel—is that the least and the last are to be treated, under the rules of the Kingdom, as full members of the beloved community?

However much or little we may be favored by our society, we are all favored by God.

Have you ever felt startled and favored by God? Has there been a time when it was clear that God was with you? Was it because of what you did for God, or because of what God did for you? The truth is that, however much or little we may be favored by our society, we are all favored by God. Gabriel's message to Mary reminds us that we are all bound up, as ordinary as we are, in the mysterious work of God in the world. God chooses us, and in the choosing makes us favored. God knows who you are—the good, the bad, and the ugly—and calls you by name. You are favored, not because of who you are, but because of *whose* you are.

There are times of doubt and uncertainty when all of us need to hear that message. We need to hear God's messengers tell us, "Don't be afraid. You belong to God—and that means you matter." As the prophet Isaiah, speaking as a messenger for God, wrote to the people of Judah at a time of great fear and uncertainty:

> *Do not fear, for I have redeemed you;*
> *I have called you by name, you are mine.*
> *When you pass through the waters, I will be with you;*
> *and through the rivers, they shall not overwhelm you....*
> *You are precious in my sight, and honored, and I love you.*
> Isaiah 43:1-2a, 4

I'd like to think that Mary also makes the connection between Gabriel's address to her and Isaiah's words to Israel. Those words are true for you as well. The One who formed you has called you by name. You belong to God and you are favored. You are precious. You are honored. You are loved.

You Will Name Him Jesus

After providing some calming words to Mary, reminding her that she is favored, that God is with her, Gabriel then proceeds in three short verses to deliver a hurricane of startling news:

- Mary will conceive and bear a son.
- She will name him Jesus (Gabriel provides the name, as he did to Zechariah).
- He will be great (like the description of John the Baptist).
- He will be called Son of the Most High and the Son of God. (He will be greater than John the Baptist. In fact, he will have a title, Son of God, to rival that of the Roman emperor, who was officially regarded as a son of a deity.)
- He will ascend the throne of his ancestor David and rule over Israel forever.

33

- Of his kingdom there will be no end (just as God promised David).

Wow! That's a lot for a young girl to take in, in one brief moment. One minute she is just minding her own business; drawing water from the well, weeding the garden, washing dishes, or maybe playing a childhood game, and the next she is told that she is about to become pregnant, through God's Spirit, with the king of Israel!

Let's set aside for a moment the shock of the beginning of Gabriel's announcement, also known as the Annunciation, to look at some of the words Gabriel shares in Luke 1:31.

"You will name him Jesus." Jesus, *Iesous* in Greek, is a transliteration of the Hebrew *Yeshua*, or Joshua, meaning "God saves" or "Jehovah is salvation." Jesus was a very popular name in first-century Palestine. Joshua led the Israelites into the Promised Land after Moses died. His leadership completed their release from bondage in Egypt. Every parent secretly hoped their son might be the one to grow up and be used by God to save Israel once again, so they gave their son the name Jesus out of that hope.

"He will be called Son of the Most High." Mary would have known that "son of God" was used in the Hebrew Scriptures to describe certain kings, like Solomon, or that the phrase was used as a way to describe those who had a special relationship with God (see Sirach 4:10 in the Apocrypha). God is called Most High in various places throughout the Bible, especially in the Old Testament. The Hebrew word *Elyon* is translated "Most High," and *El Elyon* means "Most High God."

Little does Mary know that her son will literally be the Son of the Most High. Little does she know that as king, he will one day wear a crown, though it will be made of thorns, not gold. She is there as a witness when Jesus wears that mocking crown, there to watch the tortured, excruciating death of her son. She is the one witness whom the Gospels tell us was with him from the creche to the cross. And apparently, she is there, as a witness still, after Jesus's resurrection and ascent into heaven.

How Can This Be?
(Nothing Is Impossible with God)

A message from an angel demands a response. Mary's initial reaction to this overwhelming news, even if it is delivered with the promise of God's favor and presence, is one that we might experience as well in such a situation: "How can this be?" (Luke 1:34).

"How can this be?" Have you ever wondered that out loud? Has there been a time in your life when you have been startled that God chose you for a role that you not only didn't expect but didn't even feel adequate to fulfill? You were promoted to that big position. "How could this be? I didn't think they even knew who I was." You were accepted into the college or program that was out of reach. "How can this be?" You were asked to lead in an area where you felt unqualified. "How can this be?"

Sometimes the question comes in the cries of joy—*and* sorrow—in life's circumstances. The aggressive tumor shrinks. Recovery from the near-fatal stroke is complete. "How can this be? I was told I would probably never work, or walk, or talk again." Conversely, the same words can escape our lips with a gasp or a sob. The one you love so dearly suddenly dies without warning. "How can this be? We just spoke on the phone this morning." Another report of a mass shooting comes across your news feed or television screen. "How can this be?"

On one level, we already know the answer to that question when we ask it. We know that loved ones can die suddenly. We know that tragedies occur. Intellectually, we understand "how this can be." But at another level, this expression of bewilderment may give us space to try to process what has just happened. We need a moment to get beyond our cognitive dissonance and to understand that in all of life's circumstances, God's magnificent promise is true. God is near, whether the news is unbelievably joyful or tragic. Perhaps that is part of what Mary is experiencing here.

It's unlikely that any of us will receive a visit from an angel commissioning us to an incredible task, but haven't we all been called into service, sometimes seemingly out of nowhere, by someone whose voice seemed to carry the authority of the Most High—someone, as we may have later come to recognize, who was serving as a messenger from God? Haven't many of us, if not all, sensed God's presence pulling and tugging us in a certain direction, and to a life and a calling we could have never imagined on our own? And in response we have thought or said, "How can this be?!"

"How can this be," Mary asks, "since I am a virgin?" (Luke 1:34). How can this be indeed?

And if we are thinking of Zechariah at this moment, we might well be wondering if Mary is about to be struck mute too! But there's one big distinction between Mary's reaction and that of Zechariah. Mary doesn't ask for a sign. Mary's question appears to arise from genuine perplexity and confusion, not from unbelief. Maybe she wonders if this pregnancy will occur after she and Joseph get married, and this son will be considered a son of God like Solomon or David. But if this pregnancy is supposed to take place soon, and this child it to be *the* Son of God, there's a slight problem. Maybe mixed with those questions is also a feeling of inadequacy or unworthiness in having this enormous mantle of responsibility laid upon her. If I were Mary, I would be thinking, *I'm only a peasant girl. I'm a nobody. How will I ever be able to live up to the expectations that God must have for this baby's mother?*

In response to her question, Gabriel provides the answer that quells Mary's uncertainty and fears, and steels her for her future as the mother of this child. "The Holy Spirit will come upon you, and the power of the Most High will overshadow you; therefore the child to be born will be holy; he will be called the Son of God" (v. 35). This will happen, not because of anything Mary does, or thinks she cannot do, but because of everything *God* does through the Holy Spirit. God is able. God will be with her, whatever her joys or struggles in the journey ahead.

"How can this be, since I am a virgin?" These words and the words of Gabriel have been an obstacle in many individuals' faith walks for centuries. So, let's look at the biblical background of the word *virgin*, how those in Jesus's day might have interpreted it, and how some in our modern world have lent their interpretations to help others overcome this obstacle.

Our Advent liturgies always include a reading from Isaiah 7:14, "Therefore the Lord himself will give you a sign. Look, the young woman is with child and shall bear a son, and she shall name him Immanuel." In this reading from the Hebrew text, the word for "young woman" is *almah*. An *almah* could have been a married or unmarried woman. When the Old Testament was translated into Greek in the third century BCE, *almah*, "young woman," became *parthenos*, which could mean "virgin," "fiancée," or "unmarried woman." These words were spoken by Isaiah to King Ahaz, who ruled Judah from 735 to 720 BCE. Ahaz, considered a terrible king for allowing idolatry in Judah, is surrounded by enemies, and God promises to destroy his enemies before the child born to a young woman who is currently pregnant with that child will be weaned. It is believed that that child may have been Hezekiah, born to Ahaz and his wife. Hezekiah became king after his father and brought about many reforms that led Israel back to God. This is one of many prophetic scriptures that is viewed as also pointing to the birth of Jesus.

By Jesus's day this scripture from Isaiah, as with all of the Old Testament, would have been read in Greek, and the expectation may have been that the Messiah would be born to a *parthenos*, a virgin, or unmarried woman.

Kathleen Norris speaks of being struck by how narrow and impoverished some people's firm scientific notions of the virgin birth can be, and that we can discover a broader and more relevant grasp of what it means to be virgin by looking to those in the monastic world.[1]

Thomas Merton (1915–1968), an American Trappist monk, mystic, theologian, and poet, offers one of many such broadening concepts in his *Conjectures of a Guilty Bystander*. In it he describes that which he seeks in contemplative prayer as a "*point vierge*," a "virgin point" at the center of his being, which is "untouched by sin and illusion, a point of pure truth, a point or spark which belongs entirely to God."[2] In such moments of pristine clarity, we can become entirely available to God. Such a moment was given to Mary, and it is available to us. May we all receive the gift of a "point vierge," regardless of our gender or marital status, so that we may become a willing womb where Christ can find a place of nurturing, safety, and love.

The Christ Child is conceived in Mary when she is "overshadowed" by the Holy Spirit, the power of the Most High. When I discovered I was pregnant with our first child, I experienced, as I imagine most new mothers-to-be do, a profound sense of mystery and awe at being a participant in the creation of new life. That entire season of life felt holy. I like to think of "overshadowing" as times in our lives when God's presence has surprised and overwhelmed us and conceived within us something holy. Perhaps it was a holy sense wonder, a holy thought or response, or a holy moment of calling that begged for a "Let it be" response.

Though Mary doesn't ask for a sign from Gabriel, she gets one. Her old relative Elizabeth, who was said to be barren, is now six months pregnant. Gabriel offers words to Mary reminiscent of those that God shared with Sarah when she laughed about her angel's message (see Genesis 18:14): "For nothing will be impossible with God" (Luke 1:37). If God could bring life into the wombs of Sarah and Elizabeth, God could certainly do the same with her. But there would be consequences for her: the stigma, not of an empty womb, but of one that was filled too soon. We need only think of the stigma attached in our own time—as evidenced by the notorious "Magdalene laundries," church-run institutions in Ireland where unwed mothers were treated as inmates—to imagine the fear that the angel's amazing news might have brought to Mary. The call placed on her life would be, as Ashley Cleere Cook states, "an honor yoked with struggle."[3]

"For nothing will be impossible with God." (Luke 1:37)

When we are favored, when we are given an honor yoked with struggle, when we are afraid that we can't possibly meet the expectations of that honor, we would do well to remember that *we* can't, but God can if we will trust in the power and the presence of the Most High. For "nothing will be impossible with God."

Here Am I

Here we come to the heart of Mary's response to God's messenger and message. Despite the yoke that will come—How will she explain this to Joseph? What will her neighbors think?—despite the implications of this startling news that she can barely have begun to even process, Mary doesn't hesitate: "Here am I, the servant of the Lord," she says to Gabriel. "Let it be with me according to your word" (Luke 1:38). In our marveling over the miracle of the Christmas story, we should not skip over Mary's amazing declaration of faith. She realizes that her life is not her own. It is, as it always has been, held in God's hands. God desires to use her as an instrument to help right a world turned upside down by injustice, oppression, bondage, and poverty. The struggles, whatever they may be, will be worth living a favored life in God's presence. In putting herself at God's service, she steps out in faith, just as the disciples did when Jesus said to them, "Follow me" (Matthew 4:19). Mary doesn't offer up excuses about why she is not the ideal choice. She doesn't try to negotiate with God. She answers the angel with the simple words, "Here am I" and "Let it be."

Mary's beautiful response echoes so many of those called by God in Scripture—Jacob (Genesis 31:11; 46:2), Moses (Exodus 3:4), Samuel (1 Samuel 3:4), and Isaiah (Isaiah 6:8), to name a few. She joins a long line of servants of God who when called by God answer, "Here I am" and decide to proceed with God's desires even after weighing the consequences and the struggles. With their actions they, too, say, "Let it be with me according to your word." Mary knows their stories, and when faced with her own call, she echoes their responses. With these simple yet intentional words, Mary embraces the call and the life she didn't even know was meant to be hers.

Waiting Together: The Meeting of Two Mothers-to-Be

In those days Mary set out and went with haste to a Judean town in the hill country, where she entered the house of Zechariah and greeted Elizabeth. When Elizabeth heard Mary's greeting, the child leaped in her womb. And Elizabeth was filled with the Holy Spirit and exclaimed with a loud cry, "Blessed are you among women, and blessed is the fruit of your womb. And why has this happened to me, that the mother of my Lord comes to me? For as soon as I heard the sound of your greeting, the child in my womb leaped for joy. And blessed is she who believed that there would be a fulfilment of what was spoken to her by the Lord."

Luke 1:39-45

This, I believe, is one of the most beautiful scenes in the Bible. These two women, one old and one young, find themselves in very similar circumstances. One seeks out the company of the other, and together they wait for what has been promised to them and to the world. In their waiting, they represent the waiting of Israel. In their waiting together the Holy Spirit is present. In their example of waiting together and offering mutual encouragement, they become the first example of what the Christian community should be for one another: a community that waits together in mutual faith and encouragement for the promise of what has been conceived in them.

It appears that Mary has barely learned of the good news that God has chosen her to bear the Messiah when she sets out "with haste" to visit her relative Elizabeth. This passage is referred to as the Visitation; it describes the first meeting between Mary and Elizabeth since they each received news of their miraculous pregnancies, and Mary's response to the blessing Elizabeth offers her (Luke 1:46-56). Mary could have been in such a hurry to go see her aunt, or older cousin, Elizabeth for many reasons. Perhaps they share a bond now to which no one else can relate. They will be able to be a natural means of support to one another. We often hear of groups of mothers of multiples, or cancer and grief support groups. I was once part of a cohort for executive ministers and directors of large churches. We would meet quarterly to share experiences that were unique to our positions. We would offer encouragement and support to one another in a way that no one who had not been in our shoes could provide.

Another possible reason for the trip could have been that although Joseph supported and remained committed to Mary after he received his own, separate message from the angel about the identity of Mary's child, the couple might have concluded that under the circumstances, it would be better for her to leave town for a while. The news about Elizabeth provided a perfect excuse for her to travel far from home to visit her relative.

Some have suggested that Mary set out to find Elizabeth because she may have wanted confirmation of what Gabriel had spoken to her; that Elizabeth really was with child, although Elizabeth's words seem to contradict that notion. Perhaps she was excited to see the miracle that

God had afforded Elizabeth. And yet others believe that while Mary no doubt received encouragement and support from Elizabeth, maybe the biggest reason she made the long journey from Nazareth to the hill country near Jerusalem was to offer Elizabeth encouragement, to confirm not only what God was doing in Elizabeth's life, but also what God was doing in the life of Mary and how their lives and the lives of their sons were about to intersect.

As Mary ends her days-long journey and steps across the threshold of Elizabeth's house, as soon as Mary utters her first hello, the baby in Elizabeth's womb leaps for joy in recognition of the one whom he would introduce to the world. There is no way Elizabeth would yet have known Mary's news (there were no cell phones or postal service, and Mary has gone with haste; she and a hand-carried letter would have arrived at the same time). The baby's leap reveals that Gabriel's announcement has come to pass: Elizabeth's child was filled with the Holy Spirit even before his birth. That same Spirit comes over Elizabeth as well, as she is immediately filled with knowledge of Mary's circumstance. Just as the Holy Spirit will prompt Zechariah to declare the goodness of God at the birth of John, so too the Spirit causes Elizabeth to burst forth with a prophetic blessing to Mary: "Blessed are you among women, and blessed is the fruit of your womb. And why has this happened to me, that the mother of my Lord comes to me?...And blessed is she who believed that there would be a fulfillment of what was spoken to her by the Lord." Elizabeth knows! She knows Mary is carrying the One who will be even greater than her son. Mary is carrying Elizabeth's Lord, the Lord of all, the One the world has been praying for. And Mary believes.

God Has Lifted Up the Lowly

There's another possible reason why Mary chose to travel all that way from Nazareth to the Judean hill country. Maybe she was so excited about the news that the angel had brought to her—news about how their lives were going to intersect in a world-changing way—that she just had to go and share it with Elizabeth in person. It's certainly plausible, given Mary's reaction to the angel's message. Her life not only is about to be redirected; it now is part of God's cosmic purpose. How could she not want to talk about that with her relative, who was to be part of this purpose too?

In response to the angel's message, Mary's lips also pour forth with a beautiful, Spirit-inspired, prophetic song. The song is a precursor to Zechariah's and echoes that of Hannah, another woman who had suffered anxiety because she had been unable to have children before God gave her a son (1 Samuel 2:1-10). As you read Mary's song below, called the Magnificat, let your spirit soar with Mary's as she speaks, not only of the moment, but of the glorious future as if it has already come to pass.

> *My soul magnifies the Lord,*
> *and my spirit rejoices in God my Savior,*
> *for he has looked with favor on the lowliness of his servant.*
> *Surely, from now on all generations will call me blessed;*
> *for the Mighty One has done great things for me,*
> *and holy is his name.*
> *His mercy is for those who fear him*
> *from generation to generation.*
> *He has shown strength with his arm;*
> *he has scattered the proud in the thoughts of their hearts.*
> *He has brought down the powerful from their thrones,*
> *and lifted up the lowly;*
> *he has filled the hungry with good things,*
> *and sent the rich away empty.*
> *He has helped his servant Israel,*
> *in remembrance of his mercy,*
> *according to the promise he made to our ancestors,*
> *to Abraham and to his descendants forever.*
>
> *Luke 1:46-56*

The Magnificat celebrates God's goodness by recalling God's covenant faithfulness to Israel—a covenant that binds God's mighty works of the past to the new thing that God is doing in the world through Jesus the Christ. We can all probably joyfully make an extensive list of the ways God has done "great things" for us, graciously poured out blessings we never expected, or brought about changes we had longingly prayed for, sometimes for years.

Did you notice who else Mary sings about? It's not just about the blessings that God has brought to her. God has lifted up the lowly. God has filled the hungry with good things. And not just that: God has scattered the proud, brought down the powerful and sent the rich away empty. If we're honest, we may feel uncomfortable reading those words. Even if we're not rich but merely comfortable, even if we're not powerful but more than simply powerless, we might think Mary's words could be directed at us.

The lifting up of the lowly or humble and the toppling of oppressive regimes or those in power is a common theme in the Old Testament, extending all the way to the story of the deliverance of the Israelites from Egypt. We could all agree that for the sake of justice in the world, that is a good thing. Yet while most of us don't sit on thrones, many of us wield power in one way or another. And those of us in America, compared to people in most countries, would be considered rich. Being sent away hungry does not sound like a good thing for me. It's not something I have hoped for.

But what if we look at this scripture in a slightly different light? We who have power, who have more than enough materially, can humble ourselves to bring the justice that God seeks; we can use our power to seek justice for others, we can share our power with those whose voices go unheard, we can humble ourselves and share the good things we have been given, or we can *be* humbled. You may recall Jesus's advice to people who have been invited to a dinner party: much better, he said, to choose a lowly seat in the back, and then be invited to come sit at the head table, than to presume you belong in an elevated place and be asked to move down.

There is a beautiful mealtime blessing associated with Saint Brigid of Kildare, a convert of Saint Patrick from fifth-century Ireland. In her prayer, Brigid envisioned a great banquet for the King of kings, where the "ale" served would be made from "the fruits of faith," and the food would be forgiving love. "I would invite the poor to my feast," the blessing continues, "for they are God's children. I would invite the sick to my feast, for they are God's joy. Let the poor sit with Jesus at the highest place, and let the sick dance with the angels."[4]

In some ways, Mary's Magnificat is like Brigid's blessing—not so much that the rich and powerful are excluded, but that the lowly, the luckless, the friendless, the sick, and the marginalized will be exalted. At long last, they will be treated on earth like the beloved children of God that they are.

In response to that message, which is part of our Advent story, let us simply say, as Mary did, "Let it be." May we be a fertile womb for the new thing that God wants to do in the world through us.

And not only that: let us spread the good news, not just in this season but in every season, as God's messengers by word and deed.

ANGELS GATHER AMONG US

My first encounter with an angel occurred when I was twelve—only a few years younger than Mary probably was when the angel visited her. My brother and I left our aunt and uncle's house, where we were staying while our parents were on a business trip, to drive to school. That morning, thick fog had settled in over the entire area. Visibility was poor. My sixteen-year-old brother, Mike, was a relatively new driver, but even someone with years of experience behind the wheel might not have been prepared for what happened as we traveled the winding, two-lane farm road toward school.

Mike could see a car's headlights in the distance and thought he had plenty of time and space to pass the car creeping in front of us. But as he accelerated and steered into the oncoming lane, he quickly discovered another car, much closer, with no lights on. He swerved, narrowly missing that car, only to crash head-on, at approximately fifty miles per hour, into the car that had been visible in the distance. Neither of us was wearing a seat belt, which in those days was more of a suggestion than a requirement.

Miraculously, no one was killed in the crash; I was the only one who sustained serious injury. The left side of my body slammed into a dashboard full of metal knobs, and my head made forceful contact with the rearview mirror and windshield. While I don't recall the accident itself due to the head injury, I do remember waking up in a hospital room and being told these details.

My aunt and uncle, who had come to sit with me, stepped out for lunch, and just then, an angel appeared. A sweet young woman in her thirties, wearing a khaki trench coat, walked into my room. She introduced herself and said, "I was driving behind your car this morning, saw the accident, and stayed with you and your brother until the ambulance arrived. I just wanted to stop by and make sure you were okay." Her voice exuded warmth and comfort.

As she was speaking, a phlebotomist entered with a container full of empty vials waiting to be filled—with my blood. I had always been petrified by needles. I couldn't handle it. I had endured a terrifying accident and an enormous number of stitches, my parents were out of state, my closest relatives had stepped away, and I felt frightened and alone.

As tears flowed down my cheeks, the angel gently took my hand and said, "Don't be afraid. Is it okay if I stay right here and hold your hand?" Trying to choke back sobs, I nodded as she continued. "I've had this done before, and I promise it only feels like a pinch at first, and then it's over before you know it. What if I hold your hand, and you look at me while the nurse does what she needs to do to help make you better? Can we try that?" There was something about her soothing demeanor and voice that won my trust. I agreed to her proposal and felt completely at peace throughout the procedure.

After the nurse left the room, the young woman continued to talk to me for a few minutes, and then she left. I don't remember her name, and I never saw her again, but she appeared at a moment when I'm certain my brother needed assurance that all would be well, and again when I most needed an angel to tell me there was nothing to fear, and to give me courage to face the moment and all of the procedures yet to come. Since that day, I've never again been afraid of needles, medical personnel, or medical procedures.

Sometimes angels come, not with gossamer wings and halos, but disguised as young women wearing trench coats, ready to dispel our fears and give us courage to face that which needs to be done. May you recognize those angels when they appear in your midst, and may you be that angel in someone else's time of fear and need.

CHAPTER 3

Acting on the Unbelievable

An Angel of the Lord and Joseph

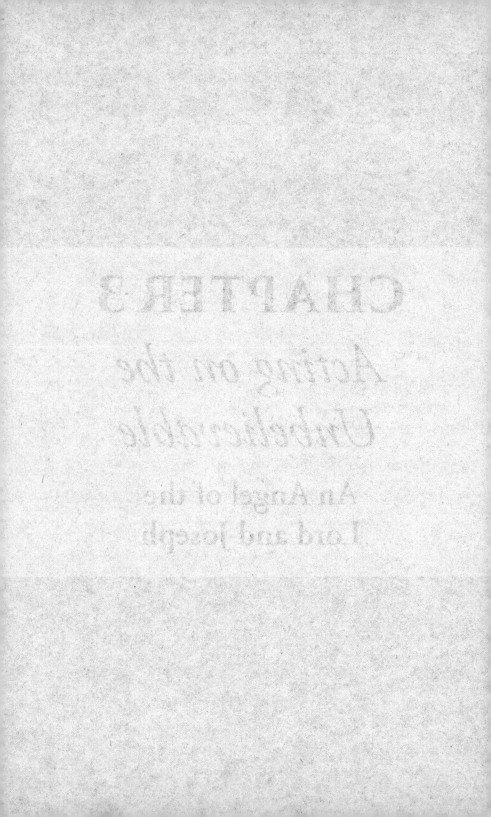

CHAPTER 3

Acting on the Unbelievable

An Angel of the Lord and Joseph

CHAPTER 3

Acting on the Unbelievable

An Angel of the Lord and Joseph

Now the birth of Jesus the Messiah took place in this way. When his mother Mary had been engaged to Joseph, but before they lived together, she was found to be with child from the Holy Spirit. Her husband Joseph, being a righteous man and unwilling to expose her to public disgrace, planned to dismiss her quietly. But just when he had resolved to do this, an angel of the Lord appeared to him in a dream and said, "Joseph, son of David, do not be afraid to take Mary as your wife, for the child conceived in her is from the Holy Spirit. She will bear a son, and you are to name him Jesus, for he will save his people from their sins." All this took place to fulfill what had been spoken by the Lord through the prophet:

> *"Look, the virgin shall conceive and bear a son,*
> *and they shall name him Emmanuel,"*

which means, "God is with us." When Joseph awoke from sleep, he did as the angel of the Lord commanded him; he took her as his wife, but had no marital relations with her until she had borne a son; and he named him Jesus.

Matthew 1:18-25

On the first Sunday of Advent, in the chapel of our church where I served the last two years of my ministry, we ask a family or group of friends to read first from Isaiah: "The people who walked in darkness have seen a great light; those who lived in a land of deep darkness—on them light has shined.... For a child has been born for us, a son given to us; authority rests upon his shoulders; and he is named Wonderful Counselor, Mighty God, Everlasting Father, Prince of Peace" (9:2, 6). That reading is followed with these words: "Today we remember the prophets of old, who demanded to be heard, who dared to speak of a child to come, unexpected liberator of the people, vulnerable incarnation of the Holiest of Holies, a new name for God." Following the readings, we light the candle of Hope as a symbol of the prophets who renew our faith and remind us of what may be.

Then comes the best part. We sing the beautifully haunting hymn "O Come, O Come, Emmanuel" in its entirety. It is a poetic, musical plea for God to come to us. Each week in Advent we sing a refrain reminding us of God's coming to us in the flesh of the Christ Child, ransoming us, giving us the knowledge and wisdom that we need to make godly decisions. We are assured that Christ will come among us to cheer us by God's justice, that God will come among us to "disperse the gloomy clouds of night, and death's dark shadows put to flight" (stanza 6).[1] Christ comes among us—God is with us, binding us together in one heart and mind, for that is what the nations want. "O Come, O Come, Emmanuel" is a plea for God to come to us, to be present with us. And in the singing of that hymn, God's presence becomes palpable to me, as I'm sure it does to many. That presence inspires awe in me every time we sing it. Every time.

That is what the writer of Matthew is trying to offer his readers—the knowledge that God has come to them. The One they have been hoping for is here, and he is the fulfillment of their traditions, their heritage, their past, their desires for the future, and he will lead them into something new and awe-inspiring.

So-and-So Was the Father of So-and-So . . . What?

You may have noticed that our reading today begins with Matthew 1:18, but the first seventeen verses are important to helping us understand the angel's messages in the Gospel of Matthew. To the contemporary reader, those first seventeen verses look BORING, but an understanding of those verses makes the birth of Jesus in Matthew most intriguing. No astute novelist today would risk numbing the readers at the very beginning of a story by offering a genealogy. But Matthew does. Why?

As it turns out, Matthew has sound strategic reasons for beginning his Gospel with the family tree of Jesus. He wants to arouse his readers' interest regarding the central character of his writing. As noted in chapter 1, Matthew is believed to be writing primarily to an audience of Jewish followers of Jesus. They are no longer part of the synagogue— they have apparently been expelled, which Jesus had warned his disciples would happen—and they are now the product of two cultures caught between two movements of faith that are growing apart.

For at least three decades after his death and resurrection, followers of Jesus were regarded as one of the various groups within Judaism, as we might think of Wesleyans as one of many groups within Christianity. By the time Matthew writes, after the destruction of the Temple in 70 AD, Christians and Jews are beginning to define themselves against each other instead of emphasizing their vastly greater number of shared beliefs (as the most conspicuous example of those shared beliefs, the commandments that Jesus describes as paramount—love God and love your neighbor—are straight out of the Jewish Torah). Though many

Christians today are surprised to hear it, the Gospels do not record Jesus stating an intent to start a new religion not rooted in Judaism.

Nevertheless, even as the foundation of Matthew's community rested firmly in the history and Scriptures of Israel, they found themselves as a diminishing group within Christianity as more non-Jews, or Gentiles, embraced the faith across the Roman world. They struggled with questions of how (and whether) their faith practices should become part of an emerging faith that welcomed those from outside the tradition, and how to balance the demands of the old with the new. Would male Gentiles have to become circumcised? Should everyone have to follow dietary laws? Had the laws of Israel been rendered moot? Would this community have to be separated from its history and traditions to remain part of the expanding Christian movement? For Matthew, the answer is no.

The entire history of Christianity and the church is replete with examples of trying to balance the demands of old traditions with the challenges of the new thing to which God is calling. The resolution of issues such as the use of icons, slavery, and the ordination of women, which seem evident to most of us in hindsight, were rife with division and passionate debate. And in the church today, no matter the denomination, there is and always will be debate over the new thing that God is doing, the new way God is teaching us to be the body of Christ in the world.

Matthew's story of the birth of Jesus, and the message of the angels in it, has a lot to say regarding the issues not only of his community of faith, but also of ours. And it begins with a genealogy.

Those Jews who are following Jesus are beginning to wonder how they can incorporate their Jewish heritage into the newness of their Christian faith. Are they compatible? Do the Torah, the Law, the prophets, the patriarchs and kings of Israel still have a place in their new faith? For Matthew, the answer to all of the above is an unequivocal yes. By starting with the genealogy of Jesus, which encompasses the first seventeen verses of his Gospel, Matthew addresses those questions head-on in what would be a fascinating manner for his audience. They would not see these names as merely a list to briefly scan through. Instead, each name would recall a vibrant story of the history of Israel and the Jewish people. Readers would be reminded of the good, the bad, and the ugly of their shared history, and that God was faithful to their family in the midst of their inevitable family heartbreaks, challenges, joys, and yes, even dysfunctions. Matthew opens with a genealogy not only to intrigue his audience with triggers of their shared memories, but also to make certain that they know that Jesus, the last person to be added to that genealogy, is the fulfillment of all that God was doing throughout the life of Israel.

Many of the names on that list—such as Abraham, Isaac, Jacob, and David—are familiar not just to Jews but to Christians today. It's also interesting to note that in most genealogies in the Bible, women's names aren't mentioned, but they are in this one! And for good reason. The women mentioned are Tamar (Genesis 38), Rahab (Joshua 2:1-21; 6:22-25), Ruth (Ruth 2–4), and the "wife of Uriah," whom we know as Bathsheba (2 Samuel 11–12). All of these women are Gentiles. They were all courageous. They all took risks. And they all had unusual stories about how they became mothers. Their stories are fascinating (and sometimes disturbing). Through trickery, Tamar became pregnant by her father-in-law, Judah, and gave birth to twins. Rahab, a prostitute, helped Joshua's army in Jericho, and was given a place in the Promised Land. Ruth, a Moabite woman, was loyal to her mother-in-law, Naomi, and presented herself to Boaz at Naomi's request to procure redemption and a male heir for the two widows. Bathsheba, stolen by David from his loyal Hittite army officer, became the mother of Solomon. These Gentile women and the children they produced were considered important for God's plan. All were biological forebears of Jesus.

When Matthew's community read Mary's name as an addition to this genealogy, they will be waiting with great anticipation to hear her and Joseph's own fascinating story, one also filled with courage, risk, and unusual details about how they became parents.

After the list of ancestors, verse 18 continues the story of Israel with a backstory of its newest addition to Matthew's genealogy, Jesus. Matthew's genealogy confirms Jesus's true identity. To his Christian-Jewish readers, Matthew affirms that they do not have to jettison their Jewish heritage. To the contrary, Jesus is the culmination of their tradition. As Matthew will show, Jesus's teachings in the Sermon on the Mount are firmly rooted in Judaism. Jesus is the answer to the people's messianic hopes for a Davidic king who will lead them to be a light and a blessing to all of the nations. He is the son of Abraham who was blessed to be a blessing. He is the embodiment of what God, through the prophet Isaiah, had chosen his people Israel to do: "I will give you as a light to the nations, that my salvation may reach to the end of the earth" (Isaiah 49:6b). Jesus is not merely the son of Mary and Joseph; he is the son of David, whose kingdom will never end. Matthew wants us to know that everything in the history of God's interaction with the Jewish people has been building toward this moment.

That is why, while Luke's Gospel tells the story of Jesus's birth through Mary's experiences, Matthew hones in on Joseph's story. As Matthew's genealogy shows, Joseph was descended from the line of King David. Matthew wants his Jewish Christian readers to perceive that Jesus does not represent a break with Judaism; rather, he is its fulfillment. So, we turn here to Joseph's story, and it begins in his encounters with the angel of the Lord.

Emmanuel, God with Us

The previous chapter revolves around the story of Jesus's birth as told by Luke. Matthew's account varies considerably. Matthew does not include Gabriel's visit to Mary. There is no mention of the angel's visitation to Elizabeth and Zechariah. He leaves out the story of the lowly manger, the shepherds, and the angelic chorus announcing the birth. Matthew gives us the story of a king whose birth was recognized by foreigner stargazers, the magi. When he relates the story of King Herod's reaction to this news—an order to kill all male babies in the area—he knows that his readers will recall how Pharaoh ordered the killing of male babies in Egypt. They will see yet another connection between Jesus, who will lead the people out of slavery to sin and death just as Moses led the people out of Egypt, and Judaism. Luke, writing mostly to an audience of Gentile Christians far from Jerusalem, mentions none of these details.

Despite these differences in emphasis, there are important points that Matthew and Luke both note, and we should not overlook them. The names of Jesus's parents are Mary and Joseph. They are engaged, or betrothed, but have not yet lived together. Mary is found to be with child from the Holy Spirit. An angel announces the news of the impending birth to one of the parents, and offers instruction as to what the child should be named. And as we learn later in both Gospels, Jesus is born in Bethlehem (where, as Luke notes, the expectant couple must go for the Roman census because Joseph is a descendant of David, just as Matthew tells us through his genealogy).

We discover that Joseph is a righteous man, meaning he meticulously keeps all of the laws of Israel. Unlike Zechariah and Elizabeth, who have been given "good news" by God's messengers, Joseph receives a terrible blow. His fiancée is pregnant, and he is not the father. We aren't privy to the conversation that Mary and Joseph have, but we can imagine that Joseph is confused and hurt. He can't help but feel brokenhearted and betrayed. *How could she have done this?* Does Mary tell him she's been visited by an angel—that it sounds outlandish, but it's true? Does she tell him she's been overshadowed by the Holy Spirit? (If so, perhaps Joseph finds it impossible to believe. Wouldn't you, were you in his position?) Does she tell Joseph she understands if he wants to break the marriage contract but hopes he won't? We don't know because we don't get Mary's story in Matthew. We get Joseph's. And the righteous Joseph fitfully ponders what is the best right thing to do next. The commandments are clear regarding infidelity: the wife is to be dismissed.

> *Mercy is a dimension of love,*
> *a way that love manifests*
> *itself toward others.*

But the letter of the law is not the only word in Jewish Scripture. The essential spirit of the law is exemplified by the word of the prophet Hosea, who declares for God, "I desire steadfast love and not sacrifice" (6:6). In Greek, the language of the New Testament, the Hebrew word for "steadfast love" translates as "mercy." But they are two sides of a single coin. Mercy is a dimension of love, a way that love manifests itself toward others. Unlike Joseph, Hosea had a wife who was unfaithful, and for Hosea her infidelity became a metaphor for the nation's rampant worship of idols instead of God. Despite this awful betrayal, Hosea says, God declines to act vengefully toward God's people: "My compassion grows warm and tender. I will not execute my fierce anger ... for I am God and no mortal, the Holy One in your midst, and I will not come in wrath" (11:8-9). God, whose nature is mercy, wants people to act mercifully. If the heart of the Law is love, then showing mercy is even more important to the fulfillment of the Law than enforcing punishments for breaking the rules. That will be a continuing theme of Jesus's teaching, and it's what Joseph practices here.

In our own moments of betrayal or confusion, Joseph offers us a good example for what to do in difficult times of decision. After thoughtful deliberation, Joseph compassionately concludes that he must divorce Mary, but he will do so quietly to spare her from "public disgrace" (Matthew 1:19; the original Greek more literally translates as "public example").

An Interruption from God

Just when Joseph has resolved to follow this course of action, God's messenger sends him in a completely different direction. As he drifts off into a fitful sleep, an "angel of the Lord" appears to him in a dream. Joseph's life is about to be interrupted in a way he never anticipated. The angel calls Joseph by name, just as Gabriel does with Zechariah and Mary, and he reminds Joseph (and us) of his heritage, "Joseph, son of David, do not be afraid to take Mary as your wife, for the child conceived in her is from the Holy Spirit" (Matthew 1:20). Joseph, in case he has forgotten, is a son of David, the greatest king who ever led Israel, the king whose offspring God promised will one day reign over Israel *forever* (2 Samuel 7). What Mary may have begged Joseph to believe is true! "She will bear a son, and you are to name him Jesus, for he will save his people from their sins" (v. 21). Joseph will become an adoptive earthly father for this divine child.

Once again, we see that familiar refrain from the angels: "Do not be afraid." In this case, even though he doesn't want to expose Mary to public disgrace, Joseph apparently is apprehensive about proceeding with a betrothal to a young woman who he can only assume has been unfaithful to him. How else could she have become pregnant? How can he maintain his own upstanding reputation in the community if he marries his fiancée after she is already pregnant? Only a generation or two ago in this country, such a decision would have been more than mildly scandalous. The angel explains Mary's pregnancy and reassures

Joseph that he is part of God's larger plan (a plan that will forever change the world). And like Mary, Joseph never questions the message.

"You are to name him Jesus." We have already noted that Jesus's name means the same as Joshua's in Hebrew—"*Yahweh saves,*" or "*God saves*"—and that Joshua led the Israelites across the Jordan River into the Promised Land in their last stage of deliverance from bondage in Egypt. According to Matthew, Jesus will save his people, as Moses and Joshua did. He, too, will lead them out of bondage, but in this case it is an even deeper bondage than physical enslavement. Jesus will deliver them from the stranglehold that sin has over their lives, from a moral and spiritual debt that is far too great for them ever to be able to repay on their own. The word for sin in Greek, *hamartia*, means "to miss the mark" or to go the wrong direction, to fall short of the glory of God. Jesus will lead his people in the right direction; in the direction of compassion for the poor, the sick, the outcast, in the direction of following the path of God that leads to life, along a path of love and grace that exudes the glory of God, a path that God has desired for God's people since the dawn of creation.

Time and again in his Gospel, Matthew relates an event in Jesus's life and then shows us how this event had been foretold by the prophets and now had come true. That is what he does here:

> All this took place to fulfill what had been spoken by the Lord through the prophet:
>
> > "Look, the virgin shall conceive and bear a son,
> > and they shall name him Emmanuel,"
>
> which means, "God is with us."
>
> *Matthew 1:22-23*

Matthew repeats this formula twelve times in his Gospel to demonstrate that Jesus is the fulfillment of the Law and the Prophets. In this instance, Matthew is referring to Isaiah 7:14, in which Isaiah spoke regarding a military crisis in his day. However, Matthew wants us to see that Isaiah's words speak not only to Israel's past, but also to its present situation.

God *is* with us. Even though Jesus has yet to be born, God is with Joseph through the presence of the angel, just as God had been with Joseph's ancestors, Abraham and Sarah, Isaac, Jacob, Tamar, Rahab, Ruth and Boaz, and David and Bathsheba. God will be with Joseph and Mary through their waiting, through the birth of their child, through the parental challenges ahead, through the threats on their child's life. God will guide them, instruct them, lead them, and protect them as the world awaits Emmanuel, God with us. That is part of the message the angel delivers to Joseph. Don't be afraid. Don't be afraid about what other people might say. Don't be afraid about whatever difficulties may lie ahead. Don't be afraid to carry out the mission that God is asking you to perform. What is about to happen is part of God's plan, as the prophet foretold. God is with you. God will keep you. God will see you through.

And that is where we find the angel's message to us, too, if we are attentive. Emmanuel has come to us in the Christ Child and shall come to us again and again through his presence in worship, in prayer, in Bible study, in contemplation, in the voice of a friend or stranger who serves as an angel in our midst. In our moments of darkness and uncertainty, God is with us. In our indecision, pain, heartbreak, or loneliness, God is with us.

Doing What the Angel Commands

I often tell my Bible study classes that people typically study the Bible for three reasons:

1. *Information*: What does the Bible say about what is happening during the time it was written?

2. *Confirmation and inspiration*: What does it say to me and the church today? What does it confirm and inspire in us? And most important,

3. *Transformation*: What does it call me and the church to do?

If we agree that in reading the Bible we make ourselves available to hear God's voice and experience God's presence in new ways through old stories, then that divine presence and that voice we hear should transform our thinking and our lives. If we are open to what we have read, we will walk away changed by those words, because out of that experience God almost always calls us to *do* something. And that is where we turn next in Joseph's story. It's one of the themes of this book. When God speaks to us, we are called to do more than listen. We are called to respond. That is what Joseph does.

Joseph knows his scriptures, but he isn't reading while he sleeps. Instead, he has an experience of God asking him to become a participant in the new thing that God is doing. He wakes up believing what he has heard, ready to do what the angel commands—ready to believe what seems impossible. He takes Mary as his wife and names the child born to them Jesus.

In Matthew's Gospel, the first human response to God's miraculous, world-changing intervention in human affairs at Christmas comes from Joseph, who exemplifies living by the heart and spirit of the Law in his disposition toward Mary, and then accepts, and acts upon, the angel's message. In this way, Matthew sets a tone for his story. Again and again in his Gospel, we see Jesus citing the letter of the Law, and then telling his listeners to live by the heart, spirit, and intention of the Law. Several times in the Sermon on the Mount, a lesson on the deeper meaning of the Jewish Torah, he begins a teaching with the phrase, "You have heard that it was said"—an entrée to written laws about retributive justice, behavior toward enemies, murder, and adultery. Then he redirects people toward the heart of the Law: "But I say to you…" Don't take an eye for an eye, Jesus says. Don't hate your enemies; love them as your neighbors. If a Roman soldier requires you to carry his pack for a mile (as Roman law allowed), volunteer to go an extra mile. While murder and adultery are absolute boundaries, the spirit behind the Law means that lust and rage are sins even if they don't lead to Law-breaking action. Jesus comes into conflict with religious teachers when he insists that healing someone is consistent with Sabbath observance rather than a violation—and that hurtful words that come out of one's mouth matter much more than laws about types of foods that may go into one's mouth. In debating with the Pharisees, Jesus echoes Hosea 6:6 when he says "I desire mercy, not sacrifice" and then invites them to study what it means more deeply (Matthew 9:13). The laws against which all other laws must be measured, as Jesus teaches, are about love for God (Deuteronomy) and love for the neighbors made in God's image (Leviticus). That's why Jesus can say he has come not to do away with the Law but to fulfill it.

Imagine how that message must have resonated with Matthew's readers. The heart of their Law and tradition has not been swept away by some new faith that has spread to the Gentiles. Its liberating, mercy-filled, healing spirit has been magnified and fulfilled—and now, according to God's will, it is being shared with the whole world, just as Isaiah declared! This is electrifying news for those Jewish Christians. And as Matthew would have us understand, it begins with an unassuming carpenter who listened with his heart to God's messenger. Jesus's invitation to his disciples will be simply, "Follow me." It's an invitation that Joseph accepts even before the Messiah is born.

Joseph becomes an exemplar of what it means to be a faithful disciple. He discovers that being righteous sometimes requires struggling with complex moral decisions and problems, seeking and listening for the voice of God, and then responding to what God is calling us to do. Sometimes that work is messy and difficult. Sometimes following God's voice is dangerous because being obedient to God's voice and call threatens those in power, those who believe they understand the rules and insist on enforcing them to the letter. There are times when we, like Joseph, will have to struggle with how to proceed when conflict arises within us between our own religious traditions and rules, and the Spirit of God calling us to a new and uncertain way of living or relating to others.

Acting on the Message to Go Home by Another Road

Matthew spends little time discussing the details of Jesus's actual birth. He's more interested in the naming of Jesus, how Jesus will live into his names, and the response of those who hear about his birth. Some respond joyfully to the possibility of a newborn king of Israel, while others feel threatened and are struck with fear.

Chapter 2 of Matthew's Gospel opens, "In the time of King Herod, after Jesus was born in Bethlehem of Judea…" Matthew doesn't tell us how Mary and Joseph get to Bethlehem. There is no mention of a census. If you read Matthew's account in isolation, without the knowledge we have from Luke, you might conclude that Mary and Joseph are from Bethlehem, not Nazareth. But Luke and Matthew both emphasize that Jesus is born in Bethlehem in the time of King Herod the Great. It seems as if wise men, or astrologers, from the East have noticed something extraordinary in the skies. Some astronomers believe that the wise men were, in fact, very wise and mathematically adept astrologers. They also knew about Old Testament prophecies declaring a king would be born to the family of David. They had probably been studying the stars for years, waiting for alignments that would, in their estimation, foretell the birth of this king. When they identified a powerful set of astronomical events, perhaps a confluence of planets, or what seemed to be the reappearance of Jupiter in the night sky, they determined it was time to set out and find this new king. They are Gentiles representing Jesus's reach to all the nations of the world. And in them Matthew is anticipating those Gentile Christians in his own community who have come to worship this new king.[2]

The magi are excited at the prospect of finding this king. Upon reaching Jerusalem, they presume that its leaders will be excited too. The puppet ruler Herod understandably feels threatened by the news that a new king has been born. He calls together the chief priests (probably the current chief priest and those who are past chief priests) and scribes to find out where the Messiah was to be born. The answer: "In Bethlehem of Judea; for so it has been written by the prophet" (v. 5; there's that formula again—so we know that what comes next will affirm Jesus's identity as the Messiah).

Herod was a brutal, ruthless despot. While he was responsible for numerous building programs in Israel, he also had many of his citizens killed out of paranoia that they were plotting against him. He murdered his wife along with her two sons, her brother, her grandfather, and her mother. He would do anything to protect his power. Though he was a nominal king, he was not a descendant of David. Reports of the birth of the Messiah—who, as he knows, is to come from David's line—lead him to plot to find and destroy this child.

It's curious that the priests and scribes summoned by Herod— people who know their scriptures and have been waiting expectantly for the birth of the Messiah—are not transformed by what they have heard. There is no hint that they react with a sense of awe that would lead them to pay homage to the one God has brought into the world. We do not read that they said or did anything to deter Herod's sinister plan to let the unsuspecting wise men lead him to the baby king. Apparently, they failed either to comprehend the message or to respond to it.

Knowing scripture doesn't guarantee that we will experience God's presence and voice. We must come to it expectantly, open to what God has to say, laying aside our own agendas. By the same token, even as

65

the wise men searched for the newborn king, they needed someone to open their eyes to scripture to help them understand their experience as a holy one. Scripture helps us recognize the mysterious, holy moments in our lives and in the world. It brings confirmation of the holy to our experiences.

> # *Knowing scripture doesn't guarantee that we will experience God's presence and voice.*

After the magi find Jesus and lay their gifts before him, something interesting happens. They too have a dream. While Matthew does not mention the involvement of angels, I can't help but believe that one speaks to them, warning them not to return to Herod. Angels in the Bible often announce significant births and offer messages of warning. God knows what would happen had the wise men traveled back to Jerusalem. God speaks to these Gentiles in a dream, incorporating them into the new history of Israel. Like Joseph, they respond obediently. Heeding God's voice, they go home by a route that bypasses Herod. In doing so, they follow God's path and purpose.

Have you ever felt God's Spirit calling you to take a certain direction, perhaps with prompting from a human messenger, that represented a detour from your intended path? How did you recognize the message as a "holy moment"? How did you respond?

Acting on Words of Warning

Joseph has more than one brush with an angel appearing to him in a dream. Matthew 2:13-23 is important because it describes two more appearances by angels.

When the magi depart, an angel appears to Joseph a second time, warning him of Herod's plan and directing him to Egypt. Here again, Matthew connects this event to the prophets of Israel. When Hosea wrote, "Out of Egypt I called my son" (Hosea 11:1), he was referring to the Exodus. Matthew wants us to recognize that Jesus is the new Moses who will lead his people out of slavery to sin and death. Jesus is everything that God called Israel to be: a light to the nations and a harbinger of justice and peace, so that others would look at how God's people lived their lives and be drawn to the One they represented. He is the fulfillment of the mission of Israel, the fulfillment of the Law and Prophets.

Jesus and his family become refugees who must flee for their lives from a political tyrant. The association between God's Son and displaced persons is so strong that when the United Nations launched a yearlong campaign in 1959 to raise awareness of the plight of refugees, several countries commemorated the event with postage stamps depicting Joseph leading a donkey on which Mary and the baby Jesus ride.

Don't we see this scenario played out in front of our eyes every day during each news cycle? As I write these words, snow is gently falling outside. The boughs of the spruce and fir trees that surround the house our family loves to visit hang heavy with two days of fresh frosting. Although it is March, the scene through my window is how we all like to imagine the perfect Christmas. While the world outside looks peaceful and perfect in this Currier and Ives snapshot of the moment, in reality it is not. Currently, more than five million people have fled Ukraine, becoming refugees because their very existence is being threatened by Vladimir Putin, who, like Herod, is hungry for power, afraid that the growth of others' freedom and governments threaten his own "kingdom."[3]

Our present world situation reminds me of an Advent devotional written during World War II by a German priest named Alfred Delp. Like his better-known contemporary, Dietrich Bonhoeffer, Delp was imprisoned for his resistance to Hitler. From his cell, Delp wrote of how he experienced that Advent of 1944 with more intensity and anticipation than ever before. He described an angel given to him that bore the inscription, "Rejoice, the Lord is near." The figurine reminded him of the importance of remembering the promises of God, delivered through the "whispered word" of the angels offered to open hearts.

His congregation read his words, smuggled out from the prison, encouraging them to "walk through these gray days as an announcing messenger," for "so many need their courage strengthened, so many are in despair and in need of consolation." Amid so much darkness, Delp clung to the promise of what he described as "the radiant fulfillment to come," saying, "It is... only just announced and foretold. But it is happening. This is today. And tomorrow the angels will tell what has happened with loud rejoicing voice, and we shall know it and be glad, if we have believed and trusted in Advent."[4]

Someone you know, like those living in Delp's day, someone facing a dark time in his or her life, or simply struggling against the darkness in our world, may be waiting on you to be a living reminder that the Lord is near, that God is always with us. Someone may be depending on you to provide the presence of God's angels. For someone, you may be a sustaining light.

Delp's words, and particularly those in Matthew's Gospel, want us to see that, long after the Herods of the world are dead, God will still be present, speaking, guiding, providing assurance and protection through the Son and through his messengers, celestial or human.

When Herod dies, Joseph receives a third visit from an angel, who tells him it is safe to go back to the land of Israel. In explaining Joseph's movements, Matthew is trying to accomplish two things. First, since it was well-known that Jesus was from Nazareth, Matthew needs to explain how Jesus got from the place of his birth in Bethlehem to the village where he grew up. As Matthew tells us, when Joseph returns from Egypt with his family, he discovers that Herod's son Archelaus, who is as evil and murderous as his father, is ruling over Judea. So, Joseph seeks a safer, more out-of-the-way environment for raising his son. Who would ever think to look for a new king in Nazareth?

Second, Matthew wants us to understand that Jesus was set apart for his role as Savior. Thus, once again we see this familiar Matthean formula: "There he made his home in a town called Nazareth, so that what had been spoken through the prophets might be fulfilled, 'He will be called a Nazorean'" (Matthew 2:23).

While no mention of the Messiah being a "Nazorean" is found in the Prophets, and Nazareth is never named in the Old Testament, Matthew uses a pun to make the tie between Nazareth and the prophets of old. As you remember from our reading about Samuel and John the Baptist, they were both raised as "Nazarites," those set apart for God's purposes, and the Hebrew word for branch, *neser*, is used to describe the Messiah (Isaiah 11:1). So, when Matthew says that Jesus made his home in Nazareth "so that what had been spoken through the prophets might be fulfilled," he is using a play on these words, for Jesus truly was set aside and consecrated for God's purposes as a Nazarite had been, and he was, as "O Come, O Come, Emmanuel" affirms, a messianic branch from the lineage of David.

When we leave the story of Joseph's interaction with God's messengers, Jesus is safe in Nazareth. But later there will be others, including another in Herod's family who imprisons and kills John the Baptist, who will again be in conflict with God's purposes (Matthew 26:47, 57; 27:1) and threaten the life of the One who came to give life. In the story of Jesus's birth, where angels declare his coming and offer guidance to his righteous earthly father, there is already a foreshadowing of his death. In fact, the moment Jesus enters the world as a fully human being, even one who is also fully divine, his human death is foreordained. The only question is what type of death he will endure. It will be neither peaceful nor natural. The creche always stands in the shadow of the cross as a reminder of the cost of our salvation.

Our Response to Protecting the Christ Child

Unlike any of the other figures in the story of Jesus's birth, Joseph never speaks. The Gospel writers record no words from him. What we see instead is action. God's messengers appear to him not once but three times. Each time, Joseph faithfully responds. Like Abraham and Moses before him, he is willing to leave behind his home and all that is familiar to him to pursue God's purposes. Like his namesake in the Old Testament, he hears God speak to him through his dreams. And like his namesake, he ends up in Egypt, under God's protection. When the angel warns him of Herod's plan, he leaves immediately, in the dark of night, taking Mary and Jesus with him. He does not hesitate. He does not ask questions. He acts.

Joseph believed the unbelievable. He obeyed the message of the angels. By doing so, he participated in the fulfillment of God's promises to God's people, promises that began with Abraham and continued through Isaac, Tamar, Rahab, and all of those in whom God had worked in the past. The question for us is where we find ourselves in Joseph's story. How can we attune ourselves to what God is asking us to do? How do we protect what the Christ Child represents for the world?

It fills me with a certain wonder to consider that the Christ Child was born not only into our world but into each of our hearts. Joseph's story makes me wonder sometimes, especially during this season, if I am doing all that I can to protect that which has been born to me, and in me, as fiercely as I would if the lives of my own children were at risk. There is much at risk in our world today. There is much that seeks to threaten and destroy the light of Christ in the world. Our television screens continue to be full of violence. Political wrangling and division abound. Refugees are on the move around the globe, fleeing violence, hunger, and the effects of climate change. Our "anti"–social media pages are oceans of toxicity. Sometimes I have to pause and ask myself: Do I contribute to that, or do I seek to be transformed in a way that brings transformation to those around me? If I'm honest, the answer is yes to both questions. When we seek to protect the Christ who has been born in us, it can't help but change and transform the lives of those around us. How do we recognize, and then act upon, ways that God is speaking to us amid and about what's happening in our world? Where do we need to protect Christ's presence in our lives and on behalf of our fellow children of God? Messages from God require a response.

One thing I love about being a United Methodist is that we have a mission statement that reflects Jesus's commission to his followers (Matthew 28:19-20): to make disciples of Jesus Christ for the transformation of the world. We cannot live into that mission by sitting passively in our pews, waiting for the world to come to us. Like Joseph, we are called to act—to *go*, to *make*, to *protect*, to *share*, to *heal*, to *embody*, to *embrace*, to *forgive*, to *reconcile*, to *love*.

God is doing a new thing, every single day. You are invited to participate. Can you hear the message of the angels?

ANGELS GATHER AMONG US

On September 11, 2001, when a hijacked plane struck the second tower of the World Trade Center, a crowd of people huddled on the seventy-eighth floor sky lobby, unsure what had happened or what to do. It seemed that the destruction in the floors below had cut off their escape routes. Suddenly a young man wearing a red bandana over his nose and mouth appeared through the smoke. He spoke calmly but authoritatively, telling the frightened people that he had found an intact stairwell.

After the man led one group down seventy-eight flights to safety, he returned to find as many others as he could and led them down as well. He made three trips that day before Tower 2 finally collapsed.

None of those he saved knew the identity of their miraculous rescuer until several months later, when stories emerged about the unidentified young man wearing a red bandana. Alison Crowther, who had lost her son that day, saw an article about this young hero in the *New York Times*. She knew that it could only have been her son, Welles, who had worked as an equities trader in Tower 2. How could she be sure it was him? He had carried a red bandana with him since he was a little boy. He had also been trained as a volunteer firefighter. She knew that the actions of the man in the red bandana reflected the character of her son, who had worked with underprivileged children through the Fellowship of Christian Athletes in the Boston area during his college years. His mother said of him, "He could have left, but because of who he was, he chose to stay, and we honor that decision . . . "[5]

Angels appear for many reasons and with varying purposes in the Bible. In Joseph's case they came to assure him that the child Mary was carrying was of the Holy Spirit and to guide him in how to protect the life of the Christ Child. Since they appeared in a dream, Joseph might have dismissed the angels as a figment of his unconscious imagination. Instead, he understood that God had sent a messenger, and he acted in accordance with the message.

One way to see Welles Crowther's saving work that day is as an act of sacrificial bravery by one human being. I see it as a young man's choice to act as an angel, someone who volunteered to be the means by which God provided a path to rescue, as the angel did for Joseph. When we orient our way of seeing to focus on God, we may come to recognize the conduits of God's love that we call angels are always among us. They are everywhere.

CHAPTER 4

Hark the Herald Angels Sing

The Angels and the Shepherds

CHAPTER 4

HARK THE HERALD ANGELS SING

The Angels and the Shepherds

In those days a decree went out from Emperor Augustus that all the world should be registered. This was the first registration and was taken while Quirinius was governor of Syria. All went to their own towns to be registered. Joseph also went from the town of Nazareth in Galilee to Judea, to the city of David called Bethlehem, because he was descended from the house and family of David. He went to be registered with Mary, to whom he was engaged and who was expecting a child. While they were there, the time came for her to deliver her child. And she gave birth to her firstborn son and wrapped him in bands of cloth, and laid him in a manger, because there was no place for them in the inn.

In that region there were shepherds living in the fields, keeping watch over their flock by night. Then an angel of the Lord stood before them, and the glory of the Lord shone around them, and they were terrified. But the angel said to them, "Do not be afraid; for see—I am bringing you good news of great joy for all the people: to you is born this day in the city of David a Savior, who is the Messiah, the Lord. This will be a sign for you: you will find a child wrapped in bands of cloth and lying in a manger." And suddenly there was with the angel a multitude of the heavenly host, praising God and saying,

> *"Glory to God in the highest heaven,*
> *and on earth peace among those whom he favors!"*
>
> Luke 2:1-14

As Luke concludes the Christmas story, the narrative abruptly shifts away from those who were directly involved in miraculous, angel-foretold births. Instead, we meet the first recipients of the news that a Savior has been born. Given the significance of this news for the world, the recipients are not the people you might expect. They are not kings. They are not political leaders. They have no clout, no special standing. The angels do not make their announcement of Jesus's birth at the Temple or some other seat of power. They meet the unassuming recipients where they live—in a field, under the stars.

For Luke, the importance of this detail, covered in just twelve verses, cannot be overstated. Matthew, who wants to impress on his readers that Jesus continues the royal line of David, reminds us that Jesus was visited by astrologer-priests who came from afar to pay homage to a newborn king. Luke, who continually reminds us that Jesus brought the long-promised good news to the poor, the powerless, the luckless, the friendless, and the hopeless, wants us to know that God's messengers first appeared to unassuming shepherds. He wants us to see how these humble people, who had heretofore been entrusted with the care of animals, now, in a way they never could have imagined, became the first evangelists, entrusted with a message that would change the world.

What's It All About?

In December 1965 *A Charlie Brown Christmas*, based on the comic strip *Peanuts* by Charles M. Schulz, made its broadcast debut. In this now-classic Christmas special, which has aired every year since that initial showing, Charlie Brown finds himself depressed, even in the midst of all the Christmas cheer. His friend and amateur psychiatrist, Lucy, suggests he direct the neighborhood Christmas play to lift his spirits. However, his efforts to create what he aspires to present as the perfect play are mocked by his friends, who regularly call him a "blockhead."

The low point for Charlie Brown comes when, in the eyes of the other kids, he botches the simple task of choosing a Christmas tree as a centerpiece for the play. When he and his friend Linus visit a lot where trees are for sale, Charlie Brown passes by the rows of tall, thick, well-flocked offerings and instead selects a small, sad-looking sapling with just a few spindly branches. When he presents the tree to the play participants, predictably, they laugh at him and walk away.

Charlie Brown, downcast, says to Linus (who always carries his cuddly thumb-sucking blanket with him), "I guess you were right, Linus. I shouldn't have picked this little tree....I guess I really don't know what Christmas is all about." Then he shouts out in frustration, "Isn't there anyone who knows what Christmas is all about?!"

Cue the lights on center stage. Stepping into the spotlight, Linus says, "Sure, Charlie Brown, I can tell you what Christmas is all about." Then he begins to recite, in his child's voice, the King James Version of the second paragraph of the excerpt from Luke's Gospel shown at the beginning of this chapter. The passage ends with the news from the angels, who, after announcing the birth of the long-awaited Savior, proclaim together that God is well pleased with human beings and express God's desire for peace on earth and goodwill among all people. When he finishes reciting Luke's words, Linus walks out of the spotlight to tell his friend, "That's what Christmas is all about, Charlie Brown."[1]

When we pause from the busyness (and the business) of this too-often-frantic season, we might be able to hear the message of the angels that Linus repeated for Charlie Brown and his friends: There is no need to be afraid, no reason to feel stressed. God favors us, even amid our struggles and our fearfulness and our imperfections. God has sent us a Savior, a rescuer, to show us the way to the kingdom where peace and goodwill prevail. And God is doing this not just for the elite, not just for the cool kids, but for all people—especially the Charlie Browns of our world. This is good news that is too exciting to keep secret. Go tell it on the mountain, over the hills and everywhere!

An Unexpected Christmas

Charlie Brown's friends learn that Christmas is not about winning the award for best holiday decorations or having the most fashionable Christmas tree, getting all the gifts our hearts desire, or even staging the perfect Christmas pageant. Sometimes, we too have to be reminded of that lesson. Forgetting that for Mary and Joseph, the birth of Jesus did not unfold without complications, surprises, and hardships, we somehow expect that our Christmases should be perfect, just the way we hoped and planned. We stress ourselves over the details. Maybe it's because we too often reduce the angels of Christmas to lovely figures in a pageant or hanging as decorations from our tree rather than as heralds to be heeded.

Christmas comes in unexpected and perfect ways... especially if we're receptive to God's messages and God's unexpected messengers.

My guess is that we've all had Christmas seasons where we were a bit (or a lot) depressed, because we tried to manufacture or provide the perfect Christmas, only to learn that sometimes the perfection that we dream of is unattainable. Even in the midst of our unmet expectations, however, we may find that Christmas comes in unexpected and perfect ways—the way it did to Mary, Joseph, and the shepherds—especially if we're receptive to God's messages and God's unexpected messengers.

Three months before our first Christmas as a married couple, Ike and I discovered that we were going to have a baby. There is something special about being a first-time expectant mother at Christmas that makes many mothers-to-be resonate with Mary's experience. I certainly did. This child, whom we would not be meeting for months, was already loved more than we could have ever imagined, and was, as far as we were concerned, a divine miracle offered to us (older-aged) newlyweds.

In our unbridled excitement, we went shopping and bought the kind of gifts we hoped to give our child one day—a bicycle, basketball, dolls, Legos, and much more. Then we delivered them to the local Angel Tree. We offered these gifts as reverently as gold, frankincense, and myrrh, because every child, we thought, is worthy of knowing that he or she is a treasured gift from God. We wanted to create a Christmas as perfect for other children as ours was in that moment. That Christmas was aglow with joy and hope for the future of our baby and our family. All was calm. All was bright.

Fast-forward ten years. Things were, well, not perfect. It was not the Christmas we hoped for or expected. Two weeks before Christmas, there were precious few gifts under the tree for our now two children. The Christmas cards we had intended to mail remained unaddressed and unsent. One morning I wondered out loud, as so many parents do at this time of the year, "When will there be time to create the perfect Christmas for our family?" Between work, seminary, and keeping up with two very busy children, I didn't know how it was going to happen.

By early that evening, the question that had been so pressing no longer mattered. I was frantically driving our firstborn to the emergency room, where a surgeon and my husband would be waiting to meet us. It was suspected that our daughter had a ruptured appendix, and time was of the essence. Things looked dark and grim. As I glanced to check on her moaning in the back seat of the car, our younger son's dirty face, clothes, and bare feet came into view. I had hurriedly scooped him up from playing in his sandbox on our way to the car-become-ambulance, and only now did I realize he was not wearing shoes. I felt awful for him, but there was no turning back.

By the time we sped up the street toward Children's Hospital in Dallas, it was completely dark outside, except for the beautiful twinkling blue lights of the hospital's towering Christmas tree, which acted as a beacon directing us toward the emergency room drive. We were almost there, almost to the lifesaving help our daughter needed. As we entered the drive, our car was stopped by a wall of traffic barricades. A police officer approached and explained that we couldn't drive through until the tree-lighting ceremony now in progress, complete with local NFL celebrities and throngs of onlookers, had ended.

My children still tell stories of how, at that moment, my personality took a major turn from the normally pleasant mother they knew to a fiercely aggressive mama bear protecting her cubs. Within seconds, we had a police escort straight into the emergency room! Effusive thanks followed. What was remarkable was that throughout our wait and throughout the surgery, I was filled with inexplicable peace. God gifted me with what had earlier seemed impossible, almost unimaginable. Five days later, our daughter was back home, minus an appendix, recovering in her bed.

The final week before that Christmas wasn't filled with frantic shopping and addressing Christmas cards. We spent most of our days quietly, peacefully, with our family all piled on the sofa, reading Christmas stories, *together;* wrapping the few presents we did have, *together;* and taking care of the precious gift we had been given ten years before. Today, it remains one of our family's favorite Christmas memories, one that we still ponder in our hearts. That Christmas was an instructive season for us as a family, especially for me. It was far from a *perfect* Christmas. It was not the Christmas we had hoped for or expected. But it was the Christmas where we found life, light, and peace, even in the midst of trampled expectations, darkness, and fear. Amid it all, we realized, God had sent us a message that in time we were able to comprehend.

Entering a World of Conflict

I believe that the same was true for Mary and Joseph. I suspect that this couple had imagined that following their marriage, they would welcome their first child into the world in Nazareth, perhaps in Mary's parents' home and with the assistance of a local midwife who may have even delivered both of them. My guess is that they dreamed of being surrounded by family and friends with all of the support, love, and wise guidance that comes with that during this exciting time. But such expectations were dashed by the news from the angel that Mary was pregnant out of wedlock. How could they explain to neighbors, who were bound to be skeptical, that Mary had conceived through the action of the Holy Spirit and that the child she was carrying was to be the Messiah? Then, Emperor Augustus further disrupted their lives, and the lives of everyone Mary and Joseph knew, decreeing that people must go to their families' cities of origin to take part in an empire-wide census. The census would have been ordered for many reasons, but the main purpose was to gain an accurate count of the population so that Rome could collect all of the taxes it required to maintain its infrastructure projects and to pay, feed, and equip the legions of soldiers who ruthlessly enforced peace within the empire's borders and protected them against hostile invaders.

Romans were fond of large-scale enrollments, and many were conducted by Augustus during his long reign. However, none of them seem to match the one described in Luke's Gospel. Augustus sent Quirinius to take a census of Archelaus's territory in 6–7 CE, but that date would have been too late for Jesus's birth, and no census that we are aware of required people to return to their hometowns. While Luke may be off in his census dates and details a bit, theologically he is right on target.

Mentioning Caesar Augustus and Quirinius not only provides us with a date for the context of Jesus's birth; it also creates a political and social backdrop for Jesus's life and ministry. Throughout Luke's Gospel, Jesus is revealed to be at odds with the political powers of Rome. When the angel Gabriel reveals to Mary that her child will be called the Son of God, Luke's original readers would have immediately understood that a conflict was inevitable, since Emperor Augustus was the adopted son of Julius Caesar, and the Roman Senate had proclaimed Caesar a god. When Jesus teaches his disciples to pray to their common Father in heaven, Luke's readers would have sensed trouble ahead, knowing that the emperor in Rome considered himself a father to the people. Even though Jesus declares that his kingdom is not of this world, the idea that there was any kind of king who might compete for people's allegiance was as alarming to Pontius Pilate, the Roman governor who ordered Jesus's execution, as the news of a new king's birth had been to Herod, who ordered the execution of all male babies within his jurisdiction. Time and again, Jesus's hidden, not-of-this-world kingdom comes into conflict with the royal authority of Roman rulers. And that begins when his family must head to Bethlehem (where their son will receive his messianic credentials) for the census.

Mary and Joseph start their ninety-mile journey from Nazareth to Bethlehem, more than likely on foot. If they were lucky, they may have had a donkey for Mary to ride. Even if they could have traveled twenty miles in a day, the trip would have taken at least five days. Given that Mary was in her last month of pregnancy, it is more likely that the trip took anywhere from seven to ten days, and the last of those, on the approach to Jerusalem in the hill country of Judea, would have involved traversing rocky, uphill conditions (which is why scriptures always say people are going "up" to Jerusalem; whether one is traveling from the north, south, east, or west, one always goes "up" to Jerusalem).

When our family visits Colorado, we often go hiking in the mountains. Sometimes a short, four-mile hike can take almost as many hours because of the dramatic change in elevation and the rocky conditions. Those are the conditions that Mary and Joseph encountered. No doubt, Mary struggled with the climb. At the end of each day, she probably found herself exhausted and worried about what she and Joseph would do when they finally arrived in Bethlehem. Would there be a midwife nearby who could help with the delivery? Where would they find a place to stay? Even though she probably received a lot of coaching and advice from her mother and other women in the village before they left for Bethlehem, nothing could replace their actual presence. This was nothing like they had planned. All was not calm. All was not bright. And then it seems that things got worse.

> *The time came for her to deliver her child. And she gave birth to her firstborn son and wrapped him in bands of cloth, and laid him in a manger, because there was no place for them in the inn.*
>
> *Luke 2:6-7*

No one dreams of having a child in a stable. While scripture doesn't tell us that Jesus is born in a stable or barn surrounded by the sheep, donkey, and camels we see in our Nativity sets, Luke does mention that Jesus is lovingly swaddled and placed in a manger, a feeding trough, because there was no room for them "in the inn." The word *inn*, in Greek, can also be translated as "guest room." We often have visions of Mary and Joseph knocking on hotel doors and being turned away due to the crowds gathered in the city for the census. That may have happened, but it could be that they planned to stay in the guest room of a home, perhaps belonging to a relative of Joseph's, or of people renting out space in their homes during the census, much like a modern-day bed-and-breakfast (minus the down comforters, walk-in closets, and fresh croissants delivered for breakfast). What they are offered is not a guest room, but the adjoining space meant to keep the family's sheep or donkeys when they are brought in for the night. In Europe during the Middle Ages and for centuries afterward, people and their farm animals often lived under the same roof, in separate rooms rather than in separate structures. Very possibly, that is the kind of environment into which Jesus was born. Was this a callous slight to a peasant couple with little to offer, or was this an act of courtesy offered to give Mary and Joseph the privacy they needed to navigate the arduous, painful, and not-so-silent labor and delivery of their baby, away from the curious or prying ears and eyes of others who might have been staying in the house?

We don't know for sure, but either way, the Messiah is not born in a palace surrounded by royal comforts. Instead, as Luke makes clear, he was born in the humblest of conditions and circumstances. One can already see the coming fulfillment of Mary's prophetic words: "He has brought down the powerful from their thrones, and lifted up the lowly" (Luke 1:52).

God chose to come to us in the midst of darkness, disappointment, and dashed hopes.

God chose to come to us in the midst of darkness, disappointment, and dashed hopes. And so, in the middle of a stable, with one last push, and with Joseph perhaps acting as midwife, Jesus is born, and all of the unmet expectations, darkness, disappointment, and fear vanish—replaced with the unfathomable joy of new life.

God never promises us that our lives won't require us to climb difficult terrain, that we will never experience unmet expectations, darkness, grief, disappointment, or fear. We are not promised that our lives will be perfect, or that we will always be able to create the perfect circumstances in which to live. Instead, God promises to be with us and be at work in our messiness and difficulties; just as God was at work in an unexpected Christmas spent in Children's Hospital, and in a manger in Bethlehem.

Perhaps you are having one of those kinds of Christmas seasons now, when things are extra-hectic, when circumstances are trying, when nothing seems to go as you had hoped or planned. Truth is, for many among us, that's what every Christmas season is like, especially for those who are alone, isolated, and without the blessing of loved ones to surround them during the season. At our church we offer what we call a "Service of the Longest Night," or sometimes "Blue Christmas," because we know that for many people, Christmas is not as the song touts, "the happiest season of all." We give people a place in the season of Christmas to grieve their losses, dashed hopes, and trampled expectations and dreams. Christ came into a world full of brokenness, darkness, grief, and disappointment. Our Savior came because we needed, and still need, saving. The Gospel of John reminds us that "the light shines in the darkness, and the darkness did not overcome it" (John 1:5). So, while this may not be the happiest season for you this year, it can still be "the most wonderful season of all," not because we can pretend that all is well in the world and in our lives, but because the light has come into our darkness and the darkness did not and shall not overcome it. In those moments when we are going through our own longest nights, we need to remember the unexpected news that came to the shepherds in the middle of the night twenty centuries ago—the message from the angels that God had been at work amid the darkness, in ways they could not see, and was bringing life-changing light into the world.

An Army of Angels

Mary and Joseph are having a sacred moment to themselves after Jesus is born, and as all couples do when they welcome a new baby, I imagine they have counted fingers and toes, and have spent time watching him as he sleeps, their hearts full of wonder at this child that God has given to them and to the world. As they bask in the glow of the moment, even as they are surrounded by the smell of animals and hay, something else is happening in the nearby fields.

For the third time in Luke's Gospel, an angel is about to make an appearance. This time, it's not to announce an impending pregnancy, but to act as a royal crier heralding the birth of a king. We've all been able to witness something similar on television, at the birth of Prince George in London in 2013. For centuries, criers announced the birth of kings in cities. But here we get a celestial herald, joined by a host of others, announcing the royal birth, not outside a palace to the waiting ears of dignitaries, but in a field addressing ordinary working people who were nothing close to elite in their society.

Notice that the shepherds are living in the fields. They would stay with the flock for extended periods, leading them to the best grazing places, protecting them from predators. They are keeping watch over their flock *by night*. The implication is that they are in *darkness*. These essential workers are *living in darkness*. They are, as Zechariah and Mary both were doing before they were visited by an angel, going about their work, minding their own business, when God disrupts their lives as well.

An unnamed angel of the Lord suddenly stands before them, and the glory of the Lord shines around them, meaning the angel's presence is accompanied by a great light. This moment in their lives reflects the familiar prophetic Advent reading from Isaiah, "The people who walked in darkness have seen a great light; those who lived in a land of deep darkness—on them light has shined" (9:2). *And they are terrified.*

I love the King James Version of this verse: *"and they were sore afraid"* (Luke 2:9). In the midst of their fear, the angel says to them as all of the angels have before, "Do not be afraid." As we have seen, based on their role described in scriptures, angels weren't always bearers of good news. Beyond simply being startled by the angels' sudden appearance, the shepherds have plenty of reason to respond initially in fear—just as the women did when they arrived at the tomb on that first Easter morning.

They are to not fear because the angel is bringing *"good news of great joy for all the people"* (v. 10). ALL people. The good news is even for them, for you, for me. For people we love and people we don't particularly care for. For Jews and Gentiles. For men and women. For those who are free and those who are enslaved. For Democrats and Republicans. For all people.

That is part of the message for its first hearers and for us. We live in uncertain, even frightening, times. Times when we are "sore afraid." Nevertheless, say God's messengers, don't be afraid. God is with us. God is doing something new, even though we may not be able to see or understand it at first. God is bringing good news—not just for some people but for everyone.

As Luke notices (and wants us to notice too), the recipients themselves are part of the message. It's appropriate, and maybe not even that surprising, that God chose the shepherds to receive the good news of the Messiah's birth. David had been a shepherd who understood God as a shepherd who cared for him. Moses had served as a shepherd after fleeing Pharaoh's court. The leadership of Israel was often spoken of as shepherds in the Old Testament. The people of Israel and God, at various points in their history, desired better shepherds for the people (see Jeremiah 23:1-4). In the birth of Jesus, God now sends news of the fulfillment of God's promise to provide the people with a good shepherd.

But something is going on here that goes beyond the image of shepherds as leaders. Shepherds were not high-born figures. They were servants. They became leaders because God chose to exalt the lowly, as Mary noted in her song of praise. When Samuel told David's father to bring out his sons because one of them was to be king, David the young shepherd was considered too unlikely a choice even to include in the lineup for Samuel to review. Moses the shepherd saw himself as entirely unfit for the role God had marked out for him.

And so it is that the most important event in human history is announced first to people who occupy a modest position in society. That itself is a key element of the message that the angels deliver, and it is consistent with the ways the Bible shows us that God breaks into human affairs. Just as God anointed a shepherd, David, to be Israel's greatest king, God chose shepherds to receive and spread the good news of Jesus's birth. Could this have been mere happenstance, since shepherds keeping watch in the fields were best positioned to witness the appearance of angels filling the night sky? I don't think so— especially since Luke's Gospel goes on to give us story after story of how Jesus consistently reaches out to those in his society who represented the last, the least, and the lost.

Then and now, the people who will most welcome that there is good news for all people are those who, for various reasons, have never felt as if they fully belong, or even really matter. Whatever it is that they have, the "haves" already have good news: friends, wealth, physical comforts, economic security, a respected place in society. For the have-nots, it's a different story. But now comes the message that in God's kingdom, now arrived with the coming of Jesus, all people, haves and have-nots alike, are to be regarded as equally beloved children of God. As a powerful symbol of this message, one that will set the tone for the rest of Jesus's story, God's messengers reach out to some of the have-nots. Among all people on earth, kings and queens, rich and respected, influential and powerful, God chose these unassuming shepherds as recipients, and then conveyors, of the most amazing news the world had ever received.

The angel offers the shepherds a sign, just as Gabriel did for Zechariah and Mary: "You will find a child wrapped in bands of cloth and lying in a manger" (Luke 2:12). Joining the angel was a multitude of the heavenly host, meaning a whole army of angels, who like Mary, Zechariah, and Elizabeth, break out into songs of praise, "Glory to God in the highest heaven, and on earth peace among those he favors!" (v. 14). Some translations say, "and on earth peace and goodwill to men." Peace. The Savior, the Messiah, has come to bring peace. And now the shepherds have been entrusted with spreading the message.

> When the angels had left them and gone into heaven, the shepherds said to one another, "Let us go now to Bethlehem and see this thing that has taken place, which the Lord has made known to us." So they went with haste and found Mary and Joseph, and the child lying in the manger. When they saw this, they made known what had been told them about this child; and all who heard it were amazed at what the shepherds told them. But Mary treasured all these words and pondered them in her heart. The shepherds returned, glorifying and praising God for all they had heard and seen, as it had been told them.
>
> *Luke 2:15-20*

Mary and Joseph had an unexpected Christmas in so many ways. Their day began with fear, anxiety, dashed hopes, and darkness, but it ended with unexpected visitors wanting to meet the Savior of the world, whose birth had just been gloriously announced to them. While we know that the Nativity wasn't as Hallmark Christmas cards' artists depict, and that we don't need to romanticize the reality of what the holy couple endured, there is something theologically compelling about these nostalgic images that capture our hearts: Mary, Joseph, and the shepherds, faces warmly illuminated by lantern light, adoringly encircling a manger overflowing with straw, while a gentle cow and bleating sheep mildly look on. And in the center of it all is the Christ Child. What is significant about these images is that they all convey a sense of home—a new home, whose center is the Christ Child. Jesus is the center of this young couple's life. He is the center of the angels' song and becomes the center of the shepherds' newest calling. Wherever Christ is present, these images convey, is home. Emmanuel, "God with us," is born to us, in us, and for us, to remind us of the home that has always been, and continues to be, ours—to bring good news, great joy, and peace, to all people. For Mary and Joseph, as for us, this really was the perfect Christmas after all. They spent it *together*, gathered with those who brought the gift of themselves, who shared with them, "and all who heard it" (Luke 2:18), the remarkable stories of this first Christmas that left them amazed.

Go and Spread the News

If you think that first Christmas must have been amazing for Mary and Joseph, think about what the shepherds must have experienced. After all, Jesus's earthly parents each had been visited by an angel months earlier. They had been told what was going to happen, even if they didn't know all of the particulars. For the shepherds, the news brought by the angels came as a complete surprise. They were spending that night as they spent so many other nights, tending their flock. They were watching for any sign of predators, not for signs from heaven.

To me, one of the most powerful parts of the shepherds' story is what happened after the angels disappeared. We focus intently (and rightly so) on the miraculous appearance of the angels, and on their message. But we should pay careful attention to what Luke tells us here, because I believe that in the shepherds' story we can find our own story, our own answers to the question of how we are to respond to the messages God brings to us today.

Notice what the shepherds did and did not do in response to the angels. They did not spend time trying to make sense of what they had just witnessed. They did not try to convince themselves that it was all in their imaginations. They did not file it away, go on with their business, and wait until morning to ask their neighbors discreetly if they might have seen or heard something unusual. Instead, they recognized that what they had seen and heard came from God, and they went *with haste* to Bethlehem. And not only that: they themselves became the messengers, the first evangelists. As Luke reports, "All who heard it were amazed at what the shepherds told them" (Luke 2:18).

The good news may have started with angels, but it was spread by human beings to whom the message was entrusted.

The good news may have started with angels, but it was spread by human beings to whom the message was entrusted. In a real sense, the shepherds assumed the role of angels. And that realization should lead us to ask some questions as we seek to find meaning for this story in our own lives. Where have we encountered angels in human form? How may we properly recognize them? And how do we as everyday people, like those lowly shepherds, become the messengers to a hurting, frightened world where so many are yearning to receive good news?

Earlier we read that God came to earth to fulfill our deepest desires; to know we are loved and to have peace. There have been times in my life when I doubted not only others' love for me, but God's love as well. That unexpected Christmas spent at Children's Hospital confirmed, as John Wesley once described his own unique experience, that "Christ 'loved *me*, and gave himself for *me*.'"[2] We may wonder, *How can this be?*

We may feel as if our past or present is too dark, that we can't possibly be loved by God until we have become more perfect, cleaned up a bit more, or gotten ourselves out of our own mess. Otherwise, we are not worthy of such sacrificial love, of God coming in the flesh of a child to give himself for us. I came away from that night embracing God's love and the peace that came with it. I knew that if the love I have for my own children is so deep, so protective, and so fierce, how much greater God's love must be for me, the precious child he came to save.

Sadly, not everyone has loving parents, but every child of God, including you, should know that there is One who loves you and *all* of God's children tenderly, fiercely, and aggressively. It's the message that God has been trying to convey to us for centuries. Even if your past or present is dark. Even if you aren't perfect. Even if you literally or figuratively feel dirty or have no shoes. You are a beloved child of the child in the manger, who came to save you, who lived his life to reflect the great love that the Most High has for all people, and who died and rose doing the same.

Let's return here to the story of Charlie Brown's Christmas play. Linus's recitation of Luke's account of the shepherds' encounter with the angels is such an emotionally high moment, and Linus's declaration is delivered with such authority and finality that it's easy to miss what comes next. Linus may declare to everyone what Christmas is all about, but Charlie Brown then proceeds to show them. He carries the scrawny, unloved tree to his backyard, next to Snoopy's dazzlingly decorated doghouse. He looks up at the stars twinkling in the sky and hears in his mind the words of the angels again. Then he places an ornament on one of the tree's puny branches. His friends follow and surround the little tree, adding decorations of their own. When they're finished, they move away to reveal that the sapling they had previously ridiculed has been transformed into something radiant and beautiful— the perfect tree for the play, after all.

What my friend Randy calls "the Parable of the Scrawny Tree" embodies the message of Christmas for me. Charlie Brown saw in the little tree something that no one else in his school could see: its innate worth and its potential to shine, if only it received love and attention. Just as Charlie Brown rescued the scrawny tree instead of dismissing or mocking it, Jesus said that he came, as an expression of God's love, to rescue the world, not to condemn it. God saw in us what Charlie Brown saw in the tree: not something to be shunned or adjudged as hopeless, but something lovely, something worthy, created by God. Just as the tree glowed brightly when surrounded by caring hands, Jesus brings good news to the lowly, the hurting, the outcast, the marginalized—the news that they are beloved and precious to God—that enables them to shine.

And perhaps most remarkable of all, the act of caring for the outcast tree transforms Charlie Brown's materialistic, mocking, and callous schoolmates into people who also begin to see the sapling's worth, and in a moving expression of peace and goodwill on earth, join their voices together to serenade him with "Hark, the Herald Angels Sing." In just this way, when we let God's love work through us on behalf of others, especially the "scrawny trees" in our midst, then we, too, can be transformed. We claim the power, as John's Gospel expresses it, to become something even more than children beloved *by* God; we become *of* God. We radiate light that cannot be contained, like the light from a city on a hill. And in the process, we spread light that helps others make their way in this world. That, my friends, is what Christmas is all about.

This Advent, I pray that you will join Zechariah, Mary, Joseph, and the shepherds in hearing and heeding the messages of the angels. May you know the love of the One who came to save you, who came to be your king, and who invites you to live in a kingdom where all, including you, are treated with the dignity and care that recognize them as a beloved child of God. May you experience God's *shalom*, the kind of peace that comes over communities and societies when people love God and extend that love to their neighbors. And everywhere you go, throughout every time of the year, may you be like the angels of Christmas, messengers who break through the darkness and carry good news of great joy to those who are waiting with hope to hear it.

ANGELS GATHER AMONG US

Sometimes angels on earth come to us once in an extraordinary circumstance to call, encourage, direct, or guide us, never to be seen or heard from again. However, we cannot underestimate the importance of those ordinary angels who gather among us that commit themselves to constantly being the hands and feet of Christ to us and to others.

My husband and I often wonder how different our marriage, our lives, and the lives of our children might be were it not for two angels known to us as Don and Fran. Don and Fran started a Sunday morning class for young couples at our church more than thirty-five years ago. We tease that we were still shaking the rice out of our hair from our wedding when we stumbled into their class thirty-four years ago. They were committed to teaching this group of newlyweds how to do life together, how to establish healthy relationships, how to raise our children well—how to be the hands and feet of Christ to each other and to the broader community and the world. They didn't show up to teach just once, but Sunday after Sunday after Sunday…for years and years and years. They still do, thirty-five years later. They have invested their lives in ours and are committed to living out the good news in a way that will make a lasting impact. We're not the only ones who have benefited from their commitment; so have the children and the grandchildren of this group, as well as countless others who have been forever changed by the myriad missional and outreach efforts Don and Fran inspired among us. They taught us how to be disciples of Jesus Christ by allowing their lives to magnify the messages of the angels, the good news for all people, and we in turn try to pass those messages along through the example of our own lives.

Don and Fran were just enough ahead of us in age and in life to have a fresh recall and wise perspective on how to best navigate the challenges all people experience in marriage, parenthood, business, and just day-to-day living. They offered wise counsel on how to fairly navigate sharing time with families during the holidays. How to keep peace in our homes and among our extended families during the holidays and beyond. (Their mantra became "Lower your expectations—raise your tolerance level!") But most important, their slow and steady drip of love, grace, and wise counsel nurtured the growth of the Christ Child who had been born in each of us and taught us how to recognize that child in the faces of our spouses, children, family, friends, strangers on the street, and especially in the faces of those in great need—those living in a land of deep darkness.

Don and Fran's influence expanded, and continues to reach, beyond the classroom. Who did we call when a parent or spouse was dying and we didn't know how we could possibly face a long bedside vigil or the devastating grief that followed?

Don and Fran. Who appeared unsummoned, offering prayers and encouragement when a child or spouse was hospitalized? Don and Fran. Who opened their doors on many Halloween evenings to fawn over the little ghosts, goblins, football stars, princesses, and angels who belonged to the more than 125 couples who gravitated to their class? Don and Fran. They taught us how to be the community of Christ to one another.

When our son married, he and his bride determined that they wanted a very small wedding of no more than fifty guests with only the closest of family and friends in attendance. Ike and I were shocked when we received their guest list. More than half of it consisted of men and women, not from their circle of friends, but from our class. And topping that list were the names of two angels: Don and Fran. When we asked our son if he wouldn't rather invite more of his friends than ours, he said, "No, these are the people who have been the greatest influence in my life. They helped raise me." That is what the community of Christ does.

Long-term angels are present all around us. In this time of ongoing pandemic and global uncertainty, we all can name doctors and nurses who keep fighting this disease and keep caring for the sick day after exhausting day. We all can name teachers who mask up and work diligently to ensure that our children continue learning, day after day. We can all name people who remain on the front lines of delivering help and hope to those in the direst need.

Maybe committed angels you know take the form of a dear friend, parent, grandparent, teacher, or colleague. What we discover is that the commitment of these ordinary angels may actually be as extraordinary, or even more so, than those angels who appear once and are gone. The slow and steady influence of these longtime messengers can produce a lasting, life-changing impact. The list of angels who gather among us is endless. Who are they for you? Have you been a committed angel for anyone or any group? Remember: God's message to you is one of unending, unconditional love, and messages from God require a response. May you follow in the footsteps of the shepherds, those first human messengers who shared the good news they had received. May you continue to find ways to deliver the message of the angels of Christmas.

EPILOGUE

Angels Gather Among Us—This is a saying that is needlepointed on a pillow that a friend gave me many years ago, just after my father died. With gold stars adorning its border, it is obviously a pillow meant to be displayed at Christmas. However, it maintains a prominent place in my home year-round. It's a reminder to me that the love and the spirit of those who have gone before are still present with us. It is also a reminder to keep my eyes open for the angels in our midst and to give thanks for them and the divine hope and messages they offer. This pillow also provided the inspiration for the inclusion of the "Angels Gather Among Us" stories in this book.

While *The Angels of Christmas,* as mentioned earlier, is not an apologetic for the existence of angels, deep down, I think, we believe that angels *are* among us. We know they are here. The late Paul Crume, a longtime columnist for the *Dallas Morning News*, in 1967 published a Christmas Day column titled "Angels Are Among Us on This Day." It has appeared every Christmas Day since. Crume wrote, "Any adult human being with half sense, and some with more, knows that there are angels. If he has ever spent any period in loneliness, when the senses are forced in upon themselves, he has felt the wind from their beating wings and been overwhelmed with the sudden realization of the endless and gigantic dark that exists outside the little candle flame of human knowledge."[1]

We believe that angels gather among us in spite of our rationality and our reliance on what we can objectively prove. If we didn't believe, people wouldn't keep watching popular movies like *It's a Wonderful Life*, *The Bishop's Wife*, and *Angels in the Outfield*, the last two of which were remade for a new generation of viewers. We believe for the best reason of all: because we choose to believe.

Still, perhaps because we're more accustomed to thinking of angels as they are depicted in medieval paintings, with wings and white robes, rather than in ordinary clothes, like the character of Clarence in *It's a Wonderful Life*, our view may be so narrowly focused that we miss the arrival of angels while we're watching the skies for a heavenly host.

A movie from 1991, *Grand Canyon*, revolves around a series of seemingly random but miraculous coincidences. A man is saved from carjackers by a wrecker driver who happens by at the right moment. He and the driver, who inhabit very different worlds, become good friends in ways that change each other's lives. While jogging, the man's wife finds a baby abandoned under a bush. Though the couple have just become empty nesters, the wife believes that they should petition to adopt this baby, that it was more than mere coincidence that she happened upon this helpless infant. As she argues her case with her skeptical spouse, she points to the circumstances of how he met his friend, the wrecker driver. "What if these are miracles?" she asks him. "Maybe we don't have any experience with miracles so we're slow to recognize them."[2]

Maybe that's us too. Maybe we're slow to recognize the angels who miraculously enter our lives because we're looking for messengers with white robes and harps instead of those whom God sends to us. And if we miss the messenger, maybe we miss the message, too, of how God is acting in our lives. How differently we might go through life if we saw

ystem the wrecker driver who came to our aid as an angel in disguise! How
much richer our lives might be if we saw ourselves in certain moments
as filling the role of angels in the lives of complete strangers, like the
woman who held my hand in the hospital or the jogger who believed
she was called to become the mother of an abandoned baby!

> *Maybe we're slow to recognize the angels who miraculously enter our lives because we're looking for messengers with white robes and harps instead of those whom God sends to us.*

As the songs of Zechariah, Elizabeth, and Mary, and the actions of
Joseph show us, and as the shepherds discovered, good news of great
joy cannot be contained inside oneself. It must be shared. Once we are
attuned to recognizing the messengers, it becomes our task to share the
messages of love, comfort, hope, and joy with others when they most
need to receive them.

Just as Abraham was blessed to be a blessing, so we are called to
respond to the message of the angels by taking on the role of angels
ourselves.

As Martin Luther King taught, we are part of "an inescapable
network of mutuality."[3] That's the lesson George Bailey learns from
Clarence the angel in the 1946 film *It's a Wonderful Life*. In the midst of
George's despair, when he most needs to hear that his life matters, the
angel shows him how the fabric that binds his community in mutuality
would be torn were he not there. And then, to reinforce Clarence's
lesson, George returns home to find that his friends and neighbors—

103

almost the entire community, it seems—have come like a heaven-sent host to pay off his crushing debt and surround him with love. The movie ends with the affirmation, first from little Zuzu and then from George, that angels *are* all around us.

The fabric of your community would also be torn were it not for your life.

At various times in my life—and, I suspect, in yours—I have felt the intervention of angels sent from God. Especially in this season, may you recognize them in your midst. May you feel the wind from their beating wings, and through them hear God's message of love, reassurance, and joy. And most of all, may you respond to the message by becoming the messenger to others, an angel whose presence in someone's life may mean more than you can ever know.

Acknowledgments

I am grateful to you, the readers, who have joined me on this journey of discovery of the messages of the angels of Christmas. I pray that the study of these beloved stories surrounding the birth of the Christ Child has deepened your sense of awe, not only of the messages and their messengers, but especially of the One for whom they speak and to whom they point.

This book would have not been possible without the amazing team at Abingdon Press. And so, a huge note of gratitude is extended to associate publisher Susan Salley and my editor, Maria Mayo, for inviting me to write this book. For your confidence in placing this study in my hands, I am truly humbled and grateful. Maria's impeccable editorial skills and biblical knowledge are always invaluable in ensuring that the words on the page accurately reflect my intentions for them, and in convincing me to remove those that do not. In addition, her and Randy Horick's willingness and giftedness for brainstorming ideas for the direction of the book and the expansion of the stories within it were also indispensable, and they made the writing process fun.

A special word of thanks is due to production manager Tim Cobb for overseeing the book cover design, the creative layout of the book,

105

and its many iterations throughout the editing process, and for bringing it across the publishing finish line. I also owe deep appreciation to Alan Vermilye and Elizabeth Pruitt for their incredible marketing skills and tireless efforts in making sure this book arrived in your hands. To all at Abingdon Press who made this book a reality, thank you!

To Trenton Waterson and his production team at Collaborate Media, thank you for making the trip to Colorado to film the video segments of the book in a setting that exuded the feel of Christmas. Your work in filming and editing was, as always, masterful. It was a joy working with you again!

I am blessed to have taught a Bible study at Highland Park United Methodist Church in Dallas for close to fifteen years. Thanks to all of you who participated in delving into what was the beginnings of this book in Advent 2021. Your conversations in class, book recommendations, and the sharing of your own personal experiences with angels who gather among us helped give shape to this book in more ways than you can imagine. I always love our time together and am grateful for the ways God has blessed me with your presence.

A mother's gratitude is extended to the two angels to which I gave birth, Caroline and James. Thank you for allowing me to share so many of your experiences and childhood stories in my sermons and books, especially this one.

Finally, I want to thank my husband, Ike, who has been like a Gabriel to me. Your words make me feel favored by God, for you always have more confidence in my abilities than I have for myself. Without your constant love, patience, and encouragement, this book would not be possible.

NOTES

Chapter 1: Standing in the Presence of God: Gabriel and Zechariah

1. Raymond E, Brown, *The Birth of the Messiah: A Commentary on the Infancy Narratives in the Gospels of Matthew and Luke*, repr. ed. (New York: Doubleday, 2009), 31.

2. "Coronavirus Statistics: USA," epidemic-stats.com, last updated April 29, 2022, https://epidemic-stats.com/coronavirus/usa.

Chapter 2: Let It Be: Gabriel and Mary

1. Kathleen Norris, "Annunciation," in *Watch for the Light: Readings for Advent and Christmas* (Walden, NY: Plough, 2001), 50.

2. Thomas Merton, *Conjectures of a Guilty Bystander*, repr. ed. (New York: Crown, 2006), 155.

3. Ashley Cleere Cook, "Luke 1:26-38," in *Feasting on the Word: Preaching the Revised Common Lectionary*, ed. David L. Bartlett and Barbara Brown Taylor (Louisville: Westminster John Knox Press, 2008), 96.

4. "Brigid's Feast" in *Celtic Daily Prayer* (New York: Harper Collins, 2002), 608.

Chapter 3: Acting on the Unbelievable: An Angel of the Lord and Joseph

1. "O Come, O Come, Emmanuel," *The United Methodist Hymnal* (Nashville: The United Methodist Publishing House, 1989), 211.

2. Brown, *The Birth of the Messiah*, 199 (see chap. 1, n. 1).

3. "How Many Ukrainians Have Fled Their Homes and Where Have They Gone?" *BBC News*, April 28, 2022, https://www.bbc.com /news/world-60555472.

4. Alfred Delp, "The Shaking Reality of Advent," from *Watch for the Light*, 89, 95 (see chap. 2, n. 1).

5. 9/11 Memorial Staff, "Remembering the 'Man in the Red Bandana'," The Memo Blog, 9/11 Memorial & Museum website, https://www.911memorial.org/connect/blog/remembering-man -red-bandana; "Man in Red Bandana," accessed April 29, 2022, https://www.maninredbandana.com/.

Chapter 4: Hark the Herald Angels Sing:
The Angels and the Shepherds

1 *A Charlie Brown Christmas* (television special), directed by Bill Melendez (1965).

2. John Wesley, "The Scripture Way of Salvation," II.2, *The Works of John Wesley*, Volume 2, Sermons II, 34-70, ed. Albert C. Outler (Nashville: Abingdon Press, 1985), 2:161.

Epilogue

1. Paul Crume, "Angels Are Among Us on This Day," *Dallas Morning News*, December 25, 2018, https://www.dallasnews.com/opinion /commentary/2018/12/25/paul-crume-angels-are-among-us-on -this-day/.

2. *Grand Canyon* (film), directed by Lawrence Kasdan (Los Angeles: 20th Century Fox, 1991).

3. Martin Luther King Jr., "'The Three Dimensions of a Complete Life,' Sermon Delivered at Friendship Baptist Church," February 28, 1960, in *The Papers of Martin Luther King, Jr.*, vol. 6, *Advocate of the Social Gospel*: September 1948–March 1963, ed. Clayborne Carson (Berkeley: University of California Press, 1992, 2007), 401.

CPSIA information can be obtained
at www.ICGtesting.com
Printed in the USA
LVHW092344291022
731856LV00004B/5

9 781791 024253